SIDDUR
סדור נר תמיד
NER TAMID

TRANSLITERATED SEPHARDIC SIDDUR

SELICHOT

עֵץ אחד
EITZ ECHAD

Siddur Ner Tamid: Selichot
© 2023 Eitz Echad LLC
All rights reserved.

...ade in-house by Eitz Echad in the ...ca.

...OM

❧ Foreword: On Selichot ❧

Selichot are a special part of the Jewish liturgical tradition. The recital of these penitential prayers marks preparation for the High Holidays. In Sephardic communities, this generally begins on the second day of the Hebrew month of Elul and the theme of teshuvah, i.e., repentance, continuing and culminating on Yom Kippur. They are also selichot prayers for various days including Tisha B'av which recalls the destruction of the Temple and many other tragedies that have befallen the Jewish people.

For former Conversos and Benei Anusim, they are particularly meaningful. They represent a desire for forgiveness. They symbolize a desire to return to the path that Hashem desires for each Jew to follow. They are recognition of our individual and collective failures.

Like many aspects of the liturgy, they can often be challenging for the novice. The Eitz Echad edition of the Selichot makes these prayers accessible in a format that is clear and easy to follow. It is particularly dedicated to the descendants of forced converts, i.e., Anusim, but is helpful for anyone who is new to the practice and desires to draw close to the Creator.

L'shalom,

Rabbi

Rabbi Dr. Juan Marcos Bejarano Gutierrez
Chavurah Zohar Yisrael
B'nei Anusim Center for Education

Introduction: About the Selichot

The intention of creating the Siddur Ner Tamid series came about as a congregational need for helping those with Converso or B'nei Anusim backgrounds (Spanish and Portuguese Jews who accepted Christianity in order to avoid death) to be able to join in with Jewish practice as well as be able to have a great resource to learn and grow with minimal hinderance. While in exile, the Sephardic B'nei Anusim have faced a difficult task of re-entering the world of Judaism and becoming members of often reluctant and even suspicious Jewish communities. Citing Yosef Karo, author of the Shulchan Arukh, in a letter to a community in Kandiyah, Greece:

"...We have heard that Jews who had lived in Spain and were forced to convert have now come to your kehillah in order to live freely as Jews and keep all the mizvot openly. Instead, you remind them of the sins they committed in Spain and, when a disagreement arises between them and the people of your kehillah, you claim these blessed baalei teshuvah are meshumadim (converts to Christianity). This is a terrible sin, because you are slamming the door in the faces of baalei teshuvah. The Mordechai (a Rishon from Ashkenaz) recorded in his sefer that Rabbenu Gershom decreed that any Jew who does not openly accept ba'alei teshuvah should himself be considered menuddeh (not part of the Jewish people). Therefore, from today and henceforth, may every person be exceptionally careful in his dealings with these ba'alei teshuvah, and never again refer to them as meshumadim. And if, has veshalom (may Hashem forbid), the word escapes someone's lips, be he young or old, let him sit completely alone for an entire day and with his own mouth confess his ugly sin. And further, he must undertake never to do so again...Written this 15th of Tammuz, here in Sefat, in the year 5328, (1568), David ben Zimra, Yosef Caro, Moshe miTrani and Yisrael de Kuriel."

- quoted from The Story of Maran Bet Yosef: R Yosef Caro, Author of the Shulhan Aruch (The Sephardic Heritage Series), Artscroll, 1986.

We therefore feel it is our duty and a great mitzvah to bring these souls, as well as anyone closer to the light of Torah and Judaism. We've done our best to bring as much of the Selichot with piyutim translated and transliterated as possible and to cover most communities. Since the Siddur Ner Tamid Weekday and Shabbat launch we've heard great feedback from converts and even those just wanting to increase their observance from all over the world.

May this work continue to help those in need and may we continue to feel the importance of כל ישראל ערבים זה לזה / "All Yisrael are responsible for one another", caring for one another within the community, outside of the community, within Eretz Yisrael, and all over the world, a responsibility to all of עם ישראל / the people of Yisrael.

Kelil
President of Eitz Echad

SELICHOT

קַמְתִּי בְּאַשְׁמוֹרֶת. לְבַקֵּשׁ עַל עֲוֹנִי. וְנַפְשִׁי שְׁחַרְחֹרֶת מִפְּנֵי רוֹב
זְדוֹנִי. רַחֵם עַל עֲדָתֶךָ. צֹאן מַרְעִיתֶךָ. אַשְׁרֵי יוֹשְׁבֵי בֵיתֶךָ. עוֹד
יְהַלְלוּךָ סֶּלָה:

Kamti Be'ashmoret, Levakesh Al Avoni. Venafshi Shecharchoret
Mipenei Rov Zedoni. Rachem Al Adatecha. Tzon Mar'itecha. Ashrei
Yoshevei Veitecha. Od Yehallelucha Selah:

I arose in the night watch to seek out my iniquity. And my soul is
darkened because of my many sins. Have mercy on Your
congregation, the flock of Your pasture. Fortunate are those who
dwell in Your house. They will still praise You, Selah. (Ps. 74:1, 84:5)

Ashrei

When saying the verse "Potei'ach Et Yadecha" one should focus one's heart. If one did not focus he
must return and repeat. (SA, OC 51:7) It is customary to open your hands toward Heaven as a
symbol of our acceptance of the abundance Hashem bestows upon us from Heaven. (BTH, Ex.
9:29, I Kings 8:54).

אַשְׁרֵי יוֹשְׁבֵי בֵיתֶךָ עוֹד יְהַלְלוּךָ סֶּלָה: אַשְׁרֵי הָעָם שֶׁכָּכָה לּוֹ אַשְׁרֵי
הָעָם שֶׁיְהֹוָה אֱלֹהָיו:

Ashrei Yoshevei Veitecha; Od. Yehalelucha Selah. Ashrei Ha'am
Shekachah Lo; Ashrei Ha'am. She'Adonai Elohav.

Happy are those who dwell in Your House; they are ever praising
You. Happy are the people that is so situated; happy are the people
whose God is Hashem. (Psalms 84:5, 144:15)

Psalms 145

תְּהִלָּה לְדָוִד אֲרוֹמִמְךָ אֱלוֹהַי הַמֶּלֶךְ וַאֲבָרְכָה שִׁמְךָ לְעוֹלָם וָעֶד:
בְּכָל־יוֹם אֲבָרְכֶךָ וַאֲהַלְלָה שִׁמְךָ לְעוֹלָם וָעֶד: גָּדוֹל יְהֹוָה וּמְהֻלָּל
מְאֹד וְלִגְדֻלָּתוֹ אֵין חֵקֶר: דּוֹר לְדוֹר יְשַׁבַּח מַעֲשֶׂיךָ וּגְבוּרֹתֶיךָ יַגִּידוּ:

הֲדַר כְּבוֹד הוֹדֶךָ וְדִבְרֵי נִפְלְאֹתֶיךָ אָשִׂיחָה: וֶעֱזוּז נוֹרְאֹתֶיךָ יֹאמֵרוּ
וּגְדֻלָּתְךָ אֲסַפְּרֶנָּה: זֵכֶר רַב־טוּבְךָ יַבִּיעוּ וְצִדְקָתְךָ יְרַנֵּנוּ: חַנּוּן וְרַחוּם
יְהוָה אֶרֶךְ אַפַּיִם וּגְדָל־חָסֶד: טוֹב־יְהוָה לַכֹּל וְרַחֲמָיו עַל־כָּל־מַעֲשָׂיו:
יוֹדוּךָ יְהוָה כָּל־מַעֲשֶׂיךָ וַחֲסִידֶיךָ יְבָרְכוּכָה: כְּבוֹד מַלְכוּתְךָ יֹאמֵרוּ
וּגְבוּרָתְךָ יְדַבֵּרוּ: לְהוֹדִיעַ | לִבְנֵי הָאָדָם גְּבוּרֹתָיו וּכְבוֹד הֲדַר
מַלְכוּתוֹ: מַלְכוּתְךָ מַלְכוּת כָּל־עֹלָמִים וּמֶמְשַׁלְתְּךָ בְּכָל־דּוֹר וָדֹר:
סוֹמֵךְ יְהוָה לְכָל־הַנֹּפְלִים וְזוֹקֵף לְכָל־הַכְּפוּפִים: עֵינֵי־כֹל אֵלֶיךָ
יְשַׂבֵּרוּ וְאַתָּה נוֹתֵן־לָהֶם אֶת־אָכְלָם בְּעִתּוֹ: **פּוֹתֵחַ אֶת־יָדֶךָ**
וּמַשְׂבִּיעַ לְכָל־חַי רָצוֹן: צַדִּיק יְהוָה בְּכָל־דְּרָכָיו וְחָסִיד
בְּכָל־מַעֲשָׂיו: קָרוֹב יְהוָה לְכָל־קֹרְאָיו לְכֹל אֲשֶׁר יִקְרָאֻהוּ בֶאֱמֶת:
רְצוֹן־יְרֵאָיו יַעֲשֶׂה וְאֶת־שַׁוְעָתָם יִשְׁמַע וְיוֹשִׁיעֵם: שׁוֹמֵר יְהוָה
אֶת־כָּל־אֹהֲבָיו וְאֵת כָּל־הָרְשָׁעִים יַשְׁמִיד: תְּהִלַּת יְהוָה יְדַבֶּר פִּי
וִיבָרֵךְ כָּל־בָּשָׂר שֵׁם קָדְשׁוֹ לְעוֹלָם וָעֶד: וַאֲנַחְנוּ | נְבָרֵךְ יָהּ מֵעַתָּה
וְעַד־עוֹלָם הַלְלוּיָהּ:

Tehilah. Ledavid Aromimcha Elohai Hamelech; Va'avarechah
Shimcha. Le'olam Va'ed. Bechol-Yom Avarecheka; Va'ahalelah
Shimcha. Le'olam Va'ed. Gadol Adonai Umehulal Me'od;
Veligdulato. Ein Cheiker. Dor Ledor Yeshabach Ma'aseicha;
Ugevuroteicha Yagidu. Hadar Kevod Hodecha; Vedivrei
Nifle'oteicha Asichah. Ve'ezuz Nore'oteicha Yomeru; Ug'dulatecha
Asap'renah. Zecher Rav-Tuvecha Yabi'u; Vetzidkatecha Yeranenu.
Chanun Verachum Adonai Erech Apayim. Ugedol-Chased. Tov-
Adonai Lakol; Verachamav. Al-Chol-Ma'asav. Yoducha Adonai Chol-
Ma'aseicha; Vachasideicha. Yevarechuchah. Kevod Malchutecha
Yomeru; Ugevuratecha Yedaberu. Lehodia Livnei Ha'adam
Gevurotav; Uchevod. Hadar Malchuto. Malchutecha. Malchut
Chol-'Olamim; Umemshaltecha. Bechol-Dor Vador. Somech Adonai
Lechol-Hanofelim; Vezokeif. Lechol-Hakefufim. Einei-Chol Eleicha
Yesaberu; Ve'attah Noten-Lahem Et-'Ochlam Be'ito. **Potei'ach Et-
Yadecha; Umasbia Lechol-Chai Ratzon.** Tzaddik Adonai Bechol-
Derachav; Vechasid. Bechol-Ma'asav. Karov Adonai Lechol-Kore'av;
Lechol Asher Yikra'uhu Ve'emet. Retzon-Yere'av Ya'aseh; Ve'et-
Shav'atam Yishma'. Veyoshi'em. Shomer Adonai Et-Chol-'Ohavav;

Ve'et Chol-Haresha'im Yashmid. Tehillat Adonai Yedaber Pi Vivarech Chol-Basar Shem Kodsho. Le'olam Va'ed. Va'anachnu Nevarech Yah. Me'attah Ve'ad-'Olam. Halleluyah.

A Psalm of praise; of David. א I will extol You, my God, Oh King; And I will bless Your name forever and ever. ב Every day I will bless You; And I will praise Your name forever and ever. ג Great is Hashem, and highly to be praised; And His greatness is unsearchable. ד One generation will applaud Your works to another, And will declare Your mighty acts. ה The glorious splendor of Your majesty, And Your wondrous works, I will rehearse. ו And men will speak of the might of Your tremendous acts; And I will tell of Your greatness. ז They will utter the fame of Your great goodness, And will sing of Your righteousness. ח Hashem is gracious, and full of compassion; Slow to anger, and of great mercy. ט Hashem is good to all; And His tender mercies are over all His works. י All Your works will praise You, Hashem; And Your holy-ones will bless You. כ They will speak of the glory of Your kingdom, And talk of Your might; ל To make known to the sons of men His mighty acts, And the glory of the beauty of His kingdom. מ Your kingdom is a kingdom for all ages, And Your dominion endures throughout all generations. ס Hashem upholds all that fall, And raises up all those that are bowed down. ע The eyes of all wait for You, And You give them their food in due season. פ **You open Your hand, And satisfy every living thing with favor.** צ Hashem is righteous in all His ways, And gracious in all His works. ק Hashem is near to all them that call upon Him, To all that call upon Him in truth. ר He will fulfill the desire of those that fear Him; He also will hear their cry, and will save them. ש Hashem preserves all them that love Him; But all the wicked will He destroy. ת My mouth will speak the praise of Hashem; And let all flesh bless His holy name forever and ever.

And the leader says Hatzi-Kaddish:

Hatzi-Kaddish / Half Kaddish

Kaddish is only recited in a minyan (ten men). אמן denotes when the congregation responds "Amen" together out loud. According to the Shulchan Arukh, the congregation says "Yehei Shemeh Rabba" to "Yitbarach" out loud together without interruption, and also that one should respond "Amen" after "Yitbarach." (SA, OC 55,56) This is not the common custom today. Though many are accustomed to answering according to their own custom, it is advised to respond in the custom of the one reciting to avoid not fragmenting into smaller groups. ("Lo Titgodedu" - BT, Yevamot 13b / SA, OC 493, Rema / MT, Avodah Zara 12:15)

יִתְגַּדַּל וְיִתְקַדַּשׁ שְׁמֵהּ רַבָּא. אמן בְּעָלְמָא דִּי בְרָא. כִּרְעוּתֵהּ. וְיַמְלִיךְ מַלְכוּתֵהּ. וְיַצְמַח פֻּרְקָנֵהּ. וִיקָרֵב מְשִׁיחֵהּ. אמן בְּחַיֵּיכוֹן וּבְיוֹמֵיכוֹן וּבְחַיֵּי דְכָל בֵּית יִשְׂרָאֵל. בַּעֲגָלָא וּבִזְמַן קָרִיב. וְאִמְרוּ אָמֵן. אמן יְהֵא שְׁמֵיהּ רַבָּא מְבָרַךְ לְעָלַם וּלְעָלְמֵי עָלְמַיָּא יִתְבָּרַךְ. וְיִשְׁתַּבַּח. וְיִתְפָּאַר. וְיִתְרוֹמַם. וְיִתְנַשֵּׂא. וְיִתְהַדָּר. וְיִתְעַלֶּה. וְיִתְהַלָּל שְׁמֵהּ דְּקֻדְשָׁא. בְּרִיךְ הוּא. אמן לְעֵלָּא מִן כָּל בִּרְכָתָא שִׁירָתָא. תֻּשְׁבְּחָתָא וְנֶחֱמָתָא. דַּאֲמִירָן בְּעָלְמָא. וְאִמְרוּ אָמֵן. אמן

Yitgadal Veyitkadash Shemeh Rabba. ^{Amen} Be'alema Di Vera. Kir'uteh. Veyamlich Malchuteh. Veyatzmach Purkaneh. Vikarev Meshicheh. ^{Amen} Bechayeichon Uveyomeichon Uvechayei Dechal-Beit Yisra'el. Ba'agala Uvizman Kariv. Ve'imru Amen. ^{Amen} Yehei Shemeh Rabba Mevarach Le'alam Ule'alemei Alemaya Yitbarach. Veyishtabach. Veyitpa'ar. Veyitromam. Veyitnasse. Veyit'hadar. Veyit'aleh. Veyit'hallal Shemeh Dekudsha. Berich Hu. ^{Amen} Le'ella Min Kol Birchata Shirata. Tushbechata Venechemata. Da'amiran Be'alema. Ve'imru Amen. ^{Amen}

Glorified and sanctified be God's great name ^{Amen} throughout the world which He has created according to His will. May He establish His kingdom, hastening His salvation and the coming of His Messiah, ^{Amen}, in your lifetime and during your days, and within the life of the entire House of Yisrael, speedily and soon; and say, Amen. ^{Amen} May His great name be blessed forever and to all eternity. Blessed and praised, glorified and exalted, extolled and honored, adored and lauded is the name of the Holy One, blessed is He, ^{Amen} Beyond all the blessings and hymns, praises and consolations that are ever spoken in the world; and say, Amen. ^{Amen}

Ben Adam

Ben Adam, Mah Lecha Nirdam,	בֶּן אָדָם. מַה לְּךָ נִרְדָּם.
Kum Kera Betachanunim.	קוּם קְרָא בְּתַחֲנוּנִים.
Shefoch Sichah, Derosh	שְׁפֹךְ שִׂיחָה. דְּרֹשׁ
Selichah, Me'adon Ha'adonim.	סְלִיחָה. מֵאֲדוֹן הָאֲדוֹנִים.
Rechatz Utehar, Ve'al Te'achar,	רְחַץ וּטְהַר. וְאַל תְּאַחַר.
Beterem Yamim Ponim.	בְּטֶרֶם יָמִים פּוֹנִים.
Umeherah, Rutz Le'ezrah, Lifnei	וּמְהֵרָה. רוּץ לְעֶזְרָה. לִפְנֵי
Shochen Me'onim. Umipesha,	שׁוֹכֵן מְעוֹנִים. וּמִפֶּשַׁע.
Vegam Resha, Berach Ufechad	וְגַם רֶשַׁע. בְּרַח וּפְחַד
Me'asonim. Ana She'eh,	מֵאֲסוֹנִים. אָנָּא שְׁעֵה.
Shimcha Yode'ei, Yisra'el	שִׁמְךָ יוֹדְעֵי. יִשְׂרָאֵל
Ne'Emanim.	נֶאֱמָנִים.

Son of man, why are you slumbering? Arise and call out in supplications. Pour out your speech, seek forgiveness from the Lord of all lords. Wash and purify yourself, do not delay, before the days turn away. Quickly, run to seek help, before the One Who dwells in the heavens. From transgression and wickedness, flee and fear the misfortunes. Please, hear, those who know Your name, the faithful of Yisrael.

לְךָ אֲדֹנָי הַצְּדָקָה. וְלָנוּ בֹּשֶׁת הַפָּנִים:

Lecha Adonai Hatzedakah. Velanu Boshet Hapanim:

To You, Hashem, is righteousness, and to us is the shame of our faces.

Amod Kegever, Vehitgaber,	עֲמֹד כְּגֶבֶר. וְהִתְגַּבֵּר.
Lehitvadot Al Chata'im. Yah El	לְהִתְוַדּוֹת עַל חֲטָאִים. יָהּ אֵל
Derosh, Bechoved Rosh,	דְּרֹשׁ. בְּכֹבֶד רֹאשׁ.

Lechaper Al Pesha'im. Ki	לְכַפֵּר עַל פְּשָׁעִים. כִּי
Le'olam, Lo Ne'lam, Mimenu	לְעוֹלָם. לֹא נֶעְלָם. מִמֶּנּוּ
Nifla'im. Vechol Ma'amar, Asher	נִפְלָאִים. וְכָל מַאֲמָר. אֲשֶׁר
Ye'amar, Lefanav Hem Nikra'im.	יֵאָמַר. לְפָנָיו הֵם נִקְרָאִים.
Hamerachem, Hu Yerachem,	הַמְרַחֵם. הוּא יְרַחֵם.
Aleinu Kerachem Av Al Banim:	עָלֵינוּ כְּרַחֵם אָב עַל בָּנִים:

Stand like a man and strengthen yourself, to confess your sins. Seek the Almighty God and bow your head, to atone for the transgressions. For forever, nothing will be hidden from Him. And every word that will be said, they are called before Him. The Merciful One will have mercy on us, as a father has mercy on his children.

לְךָ אֲדֹנָי הַצְּדָקָה. וְלָנוּ בֹּשֶׁת הַפָּנִים:

Lecha Adonai Hatzedakah. Velanu Boshet Hapanim:

To You, Hashem, is righteousness, and to us is the shame of our faces.

Mah Nit'onen Umah Nomar.	מַה נִּתְאוֹנֵן וּמַה נֹּאמַר.
Mah Nedaber Umah Nitztaddak:	מַה נְּדַבֵּר וּמַה נִּצְטַדָּק:
Nachpesah Deracheinu	נַחְפְּשָׂה דְרָכֵינוּ
Venachkorah. Venashuvah	וְנַחְקֹרָה. וְנָשׁוּבָה
Eleicha: Ki Yemincha Peshutah.	אֵלֶיךָ: כִּי יְמִינְךָ פְּשׁוּטָה.
Lekabel Shavim: Shavim Eleicha	לְקַבֵּל שָׁבִים: שָׁבִים אֵלֶיךָ
Bechol Lev. Shav'atam Tekabel	בְּכָל לֵב. שַׁוְעָתָם תְּקַבֵּל
Berachameicha: Berachameicha	בְּרַחֲמֶיךָ: בְּרַחֲמֶיךָ
Harabbim Banu Lefaneicha.	הָרַבִּים בָּאנוּ לְפָנֶיךָ.
Kedallim Ucherashim Dafaknu	כְּדַלִּים וּכְרָשִׁים דָּפַקְנוּ
Delateicha: Delateicha Dafaknu	דְּלָתֶיךָ: דְּלָתֶיךָ דָּפַקְנוּ

Rachum Vechanun. Al Teshivenu   רַחוּם וְחַנּוּן. אַל תְּשִׁיבֵנוּ

Reikam Millefaneicha: רֵיקָם מִלְּפָנֶיךָ:

Millefaneicha Malkenu Reikam   מִלְּפָנֶיךָ מַלְכֵּנוּ רֵיקָם

Al Teshivenu. Ki Attah Shomea'   אַל תְּשִׁיבֵנוּ. כִּי אַתָּה שׁוֹמֵעַ

Tefillah: Shomea' Tefillah.   תְּפִלָּה: שׁוֹמֵעַ תְּפִלָּה.

Adeicha Kol Basar Yavo'u: עָדֶיךָ כָּל בָּשָׂר יָבֹאוּ:

Shomea' Techinah. Eleicha Kol   שׁוֹמֵעַ תְּחִנָּה. אֵלֶיךָ כָּל

Haruchot Yavo'u: Yavo'u Eleicha   הָרוּחוֹת יָבֹאוּ: יָבֹאוּ אֵלֶיךָ

Haruchot. Vechol Haneshamah: הָרוּחוֹת. וְכָל הַנְּשָׁמָה:

What shall we complain about and what shall we say? What shall we speak and how shall we be justified? Let us search our ways and investigate them, and we shall return to You; for Your right hand is outstretched to accept those who return, returning to You with all their heart. You will accept their cry with Your mercy; with Your abundant mercy, we come before You. Like the poor and the destitute, we knock on Your doors; we knock on Your doors, merciful and gracious One. Do not send us away empty-handed from Your presence; from Your presence, our King, do not send us away empty-handed. For You hear the prayer; You hear the prayer. All flesh will come to You; You hear the supplication. To You, all the spirits will come; the spirits will come to You. And every soul.

Haneshamah Lach

Haneshamah Lach Vehaguf   הַנְּשָׁמָה לָךְ וְהַגּוּף

Po'olach. Chusah Al Amalach: פָּעֳלָךְ. חוּסָה עַל עֲמָלָךְ:

Haneshamah Lach Vehaguf   הַנְּשָׁמָה לָךְ וְהַגּוּף

Po'olach. Tzur Asher Ein Domeh   פָּעֳלָךְ. צוּר אֲשֶׁר אֵין דּוֹמֶה

Lach. Chusah Al Amalach: לָךְ. חוּסָה עַל עֲמָלָךְ:

Haneshamah Lach Vehaguf	הַנְּשָׁמָה לָךְ וְהַגּוּף
Po'olach. Adonai Aseh Lema'an	פָּעֳלָךְ. יְהֹוָה עֲשֵׂה לְמַעַן
Shimcha: Atanu Al Shimcha.	שְׁמֶךָ: אָתָאנוּ עַל שְׁמֶךָ.
Adonai Aseh Lema'an Shimcha:	יְהֹוָה עֲשֵׂה לְמַעַן שְׁמֶךָ:
Ba'avur Shimcha. Ki El Melech	בַּעֲבוּר שְׁמֶךָ. כִּי אֵל מֶלֶךְ
Chanun Verachum Shemecha:	חַנּוּן וְרַחוּם שְׁמֶךָ:
Shimcha Nikra Aleinu. Adonai	שִׁמְךָ נִקְרָא עָלֵינוּ. יְהֹוָה
Eloheinu: Shimcha Nikra	אֱלֹהֵינוּ: שִׁמְךָ נִקְרָא
Bekirbenu. Al Tanichenu Adonai	בְּקִרְבֵּנוּ. אַל תַּנִּיחֵנוּ יְהֹוָה
Eloheinu: Eloheinu Boshenu	אֱלֹהֵינוּ: אֱלֹהֵינוּ בֹּשְׁנוּ
Bema'aseinu. Venichlamnu	בְּמַעֲשֵׂינוּ. וְנִכְלַמְנוּ
Ba'avonoteinu: Ein Lanu Peh	בַּעֲוֹנוֹתֵינוּ: אֵין לָנוּ פֶּה
Lehashiv. Velo Metzach Leharim	לְהָשִׁיב. וְלֹא מֵצַח לְהָרִים
Rosh: Ki Rabu Meshuvoteinu.	רֹאשׁ: כִּי רַבּוּ מְשׁוּבוֹתֵינוּ.
Lecha Chatanu: Chatanu Im	לְךָ חָטָאנוּ: חָטָאנוּ עִם
Avoteinu. He'evinu Hirsha'enu:	אֲבוֹתֵינוּ. הֶעֱוִינוּ הִרְשַׁעְנוּ:
Mah Nomar Lefaneicha Adonai	מַה נֹּאמַר לְפָנֶיךָ יְהֹוָה
Eloheinu. Mah Nedaber Umah	אֱלֹהֵינוּ. מַה נְּדַבֵּר וּמַה
Nitztaddak:	נִּצְטַדָּק:

The soul is Yours and the body is Your handiwork. Have pity on Your handiwork; the soul is Yours and the body is Your handiwork. Rock, there is none like You. Have pity on Your handiwork; the soul is Yours and the body is Your handiwork. Hashem, act for the sake of Your Name; we come to You for Your Name. Hashem, act for the sake of Your Name; for the sake of Your Name. For Your Name is called the merciful and gracious King; Your Name is called upon us. Hashem our God; Your Name is called within us. Do not forsake us, Hashem our God; our God, we are ashamed of our deeds. And we are confounded by our iniquities. We have no mouth to answer, nor a reason to raise our heads; for our backslidings have increased. We have sinned against You; we have sinned with our fathers. We have acted perversely, we have done wickedly; what shall we say before You, Hashem our God? What shall we speak and how shall we be justified?

Mah Nomar Lefaneicha

Mah Nomar Lefaneicha Yoshev	מַה נֹּאמַר לְפָנֶיךָ יוֹשֵׁב
Marom. Umah Nesaper	מָרוֹם. וּמַה נְּסַפֵּר
Lefaneicha Shochen Shechakim:	לְפָנֶיךָ שׁוֹכֵן שְׁחָקִים:
Halo Hanistarot Vehaniglot.	הֲלֹא הַנִּסְתָּרוֹת וְהַנִּגְלוֹת.
Attah Yodea': Attah Yodea' Razei	אַתָּה יוֹדֵעַ: אַתָּה יוֹדֵעַ רָזֵי
Olam. Veta'alumot Sitrei Chol	עוֹלָם. וְתַעֲלוּמוֹת סִתְרֵי כָל
Chai: Attah Chofes Kol Chadrei	חָי: אַתָּה חוֹפֵשׂ כָּל חַדְרֵי
Vaten. Ro'eh Chelayot Valev:	בָטֶן. רוֹאֶה כְלָיוֹת וָלֵב:
Ein Davar Ne'lam Mimach.	אֵין דָּבָר נֶעְלָם מִמָּךְ. וְאֵין
Ve'ein Nistar Mineged Eineicha:	נִסְתָּר מִנֶּגֶד עֵינֶיךָ:

What shall we say before You, Oh You who sits on high? And what shall we recount before You, Oh You who dwells in the heavens? Certainly You know the hidden and the revealed [things]. You know the mysteries of the universe, and the secrets of all living things; You search all the chambers of the womb. Seeing the kidneys and the heart; there is nothing hidden from You. And there is nothing concealed from before Your eyes.

Im Avoneinu

Im Avoneinu Anu Vanu. Adonai	אִם עֲוֹנֵינוּ עָנוּ בָנוּ. יְהֹוָה
Aseh Lema'an Shemecha: Im	עֲשֵׂה לְמַעַן שְׁמֶךָ: אִם
Avonot Tishmar Yah. Adonai Mi	עֲוֹנוֹת תִּשְׁמָר יָהּ. אֲדֹנָי מִי
Ya'amod: Ki Imecha	יַעֲמֹד: כִּי עִמְּךָ
Hasselichah. Lema'an Tivare: Ki	הַסְּלִיחָה. לְמַעַן תִּוָּרֵא: כִּי
Imecha Mekor Chayim.	עִמְּךָ מְקוֹר חַיִּים.
Be'orecha Nir'eh Or: Ki Lo Al	בְּאוֹרְךָ נִרְאֶה אוֹר: כִּי לֹא עַל
Tzidkoteinu Anachnu Mapilim	צִדְקוֹתֵינוּ אֲנַחְנוּ מַפִּילִים
Tachanuneinu Lefaneicha. Ki Al	תַּחֲנוּנֵינוּ לְפָנֶיךָ. כִּי עַל
Rachameicha Harabbim:	רַחֲמֶיךָ הָרַבִּים:

If our iniquities testify against us, Oh Hashem, act for the sake of Your Name. If You keep iniquities, Oh Hashem. Hashem, who can stand? For with You is forgiveness. So that You may be feared. For with You is the fountain of life. In Your light, we see light. For it is not on account of our righteousness that we cast our supplications before You. But on account of Your abundant mercy.

Some add this only during the Ten Days of Repentance (Yom Kippur to Rosh Hashanah):

Lema'ancha Elohai. Retzeh Am	לְמַעַנְךָ אֱלֹהַי. רְצֵה עַם
Lecha Shichar. Lechallot	לְךָ שִׁחַר. לְחַלּוֹת
Paneicha. Bema'amad	פָּנֶיךָ. בְּמַעֲמַד
Hashachar. Adonai Hakshivah	הַשַּׁחַר. אֲדֹנָי הַקְשִׁיבָה
Va'aseh Al Te'achar:	וַעֲשֵׂה אַל תְּאַחַר:

For your sake, my God. Be pleased with a people who seek You at dawn. To entreat Your presence at the break of dawn. Hashem, listen and act, do not delay.

Lema'ancha Elohai. Deleh	לְמַעַנְךָ אֱלֹהַי. דְּלֵה
Mimetzulot Yam. Seve'ei Rosh	מִמְּצֻלוֹת יָם. שְׂבֵעֵי רֹאשׁ
Vela'an. Beveit Nodam	וְלַעַן. בְּבֵית נוֹדָם
Veshivyam. Veshur Lachtzam	וְשִׁבְיָם. וְשׁוּר לַחְצָם
Ve'onyam. Ve'al Tefen	וְעָנְיָם. וְאַל תֵּפֶן
Lemeryam. Vehat Ozen	לְמֶרְיָם. וְהַט אֹזֶן
Leshav'am. Bitfillat Hashachar:	לְשַׁוְעָם. בִּתְפִלַּת הַשַּׁחַר:
Adonai Hakshivah Va'aseh Al	אֲדֹנָי הַקְשִׁיבָה וַעֲשֵׂה אַל
Te'achar:	תְּאַחַר:

For Your sake, my God. Deliver from the depths of the sea. Those sated with poverty and wormwood. In the house of those who slumber and are captive. And support the oppressed and the poor. And do not turn to the rebellious. Incline your ear to their cries. In the morning prayer: Hashem, listen and act, do not delay.

Lema'ancha Elohai. Va'aseh	לְמַעַנְךָ אֱלֹהַי. וַעֲשֵׂה
Letovah Ot. Vechon Nefashot	לְטוֹבָה אוֹת. וְחֹן נְפָשׁוֹת
Atzuvot. Lemei Yesha Tzeme'ot.	עֲצוּבוֹת. לְמֵי יֶשַׁע צְמֵאוֹת.
Vekabetz Niddachim. Pezurim	וְקַבֵּץ נִדָּחִים. פְּזוּרִים
Bechol Pe'ot. Asher Merov	בְּכָל פֵּאוֹת. אֲשֶׁר מֵרֹב
Tela'ot. Oram Me'od Shachar:	תְּלָאוֹת. עוֹרָם מְאֹד שָׁחַר:
Adonai Hakshivah Va'aseh Al	אֲדֹנָי הַקְשִׁיבָה וַעֲשֵׂה אַל
Te'achar:	תְּאַחַר:

For Your sake, my God. Do good and show favor to the downcast souls. For the waters of salvation, they thirst. Gather those that are scattered, dispersed in all corners who are in great distress. Their cries rise early: Hashem, listen and act, do not delay.

Lema'ancha Elohai. Yehemu	לְמַעַנְךָ אֱלֹהָי. יֶהֱמוּ
Rachameicha. Umime'on	רַחֲמֶיךָ. וּמִמְּעוֹן
Shameicha. Shema Kol	שָׁמֶיךָ. שְׁמַע קוֹל
Ammecha. Sovelei Apecha.	עַמֶּךָ. סוֹבְלֵי אַפֶּךָ.
Kitzpecha Veza'amecha.	קִצְפְּךָ וְזַעֲמֶךָ.
Umineso Eimeicha. Libam	וּמִנְּשׂוֹא אֵימֶיךָ. לִבָּם
Me'od Secharchar: Adonai	מְאֹד סְחַרְחַר: אֲדֹנָי
Hakshivah Va'aseh Al Te'achar:	הַקְשִׁיבָה וַעֲשֵׂה אַל תְּאַחַר:

For Your sake, my God. Let your compassion stir and from the dwelling of the heavens, hear the voice of your people. Those who suffer your wrath, anger, and fury. And from the height of your awe, their hearts are greatly troubled: Hashem, listen and act, do not delay.

Lema'ancha Elohai. Dalleicha	לְמַעַנְךָ אֱלֹהָי. דַּלֶּיךָ
Terachem. Vesamechem	תְּרַחֵם. וְשַׂמְּחֵם
Migonam. Uva'atzatecha	מִיגוֹנָם. וּבַעֲצָתְךָ
Tanchem. Vehafle Chasadeicha.	תַנְחֵם. וְהַפְלֵא חֲסָדֶיךָ.
Vechusah Na Verachem.	וְחוּסָה נָא וְרַחֵם.
Amusim Mibeten Umerechem	עֲמוּסִים מִבֶּטֶן וּמֵרֶחֶם
Mishchar. Adonai Hakshivah	מִשָּׁחַר. אֲדֹנָי הַקְשִׁיבָה
Va'aseh Al Te'achar:	וַעֲשֵׂה אַל תְּאַחַר:

For Your sake, my God. Show mercy to the needy and cheer them from their sorrow. Comfort them with your counsel and perform wonders with your loving-kindness. Please have pity and compassion. Hidden from the womb and from the dawn, Hashem, listen and act, do not delay.

End of section.

Adonai Shema'ah

Adonai, Shema'ah. Adonai,	אֲדֹנָי. שְׁמָעָה. אֲדֹנָי.
Selachah. Adonai Hakshivah	סְלָחָה. אֲדֹנָי הַקְשִׁיבָה
Va'aseh Al Te'achar,	וַעֲשֵׂה אַל תְּאַחַר.
Lema'ancha Elohai Ki Shimcha	לְמַעַנְךָ אֱלֹהַי כִּי שִׁמְךָ
Nikra Al Ircha Ve'al Ammecha:	נִקְרָא עַל עִירְךָ וְעַל עַמֶּךָ:
Hashivenu Adonai Eleicha	הֲשִׁיבֵנוּ יְהוָה אֵלֶיךָ
Venashuvah. Chadesh Yameinu	וְנָשׁוּבָה. חַדֵּשׁ יָמֵינוּ
Kekedem:	כְּקֶדֶם:

Hashem, hear. Hashem, forgive. Hashem, listen and act, do not delay, for Your sake, my God, for Your name is called upon Your city and Your people: Restore us, Hashem, and we shall return. Renew our days as of old.

Some congregations say the following piyut:

יְהוָה אֱלֹהֵי הַצְּבָאוֹת יוֹשֵׁב הַכְּרוּבִים. בָּטִית לְעַמְּךָ שׁוּבוּ בָנִים
שׁוֹבָבִים. גְּשׁוּ נָא אֵלַי בִּדְבָרִים עֲרֵבִים. דְּרָשׁוּנִי וִחְיוּ יָמִים רַבִּים.
הֲלֹא דְבָרֶיךָ לְעוֹלָם נִצָּבִים. וּבָם אֲנַחְנוּ נִשְׁעָנִים וְנִקְרָבִים. זָכְרֵנוּ
לְחַיִּים טוֹבִים. חָנֵּנוּ בַּחֲסָדֶיךָ הָרַבִּים. טוֹב אַתָּה לָרָעִים וְלַטּוֹבִים.
יְמִינְךָ פְּשׁוּטָה לְקַבֵּל שָׁבִים. כִּי לֹא תַחְפֹּץ בְּמִיתַת חַיָּבִים. לָכֵן
אֲנַחְנוּ מַשְׁכִּימִים וּמַעֲרִיבִים. מֶלֶךְ מְהֻלָּל בְּמַחֲנוֹת כְּרוּבִים. נַקֵּנוּ
מֵחֵטְא וּמִכָּל חַיּוּבִים. סְלַח לָנוּ כִּי פְּשָׁעֵינוּ מְרֻבִּים. עֲנֵנוּ לְמַעַן
צוּרִים הַחֲצוּבִים. פִּתְחֵי תְשׁוּבָה בַּל יִהְיוּ מְשֻׁלָּבִים. צַעֲקוֹתֵינוּ
לְפָנֶיךָ יִהְיוּ נִקְרָבִים. קָרְבֵּנוּ אֵלֶיךָ חוֹצֵב לְהָבִים. רְצֵנוּ כְּעוֹלוֹת
פָּרִים וּכְשָׁבִים. שַׁבֵנוּ אֵלֶיךָ נְעָרִים וְשָׁבִים. תְּמוּכִים בְּטוּחִים עַל
רַחֲמֶיךָ הָרַבִּים. רַחֵם תְּרַחֵם עָלֵינוּ צוּר שׁוֹכֵן מְרוֹמִים. אֵל מֶלֶךְ
יוֹשֵׁב עַל כִּסֵּא רַחֲמִים:

Adonai Elohei Hatzeva'ot Yoshev Hakeruvim. Batit Le'ammecha Shuvu Banim Shovavim. Geshu Na Elai Bidvarim Arevim. Dirshuni Vichyu Yamim Rabbim. Halo Devareicha Le'olam Nitzavim. Uvam Anachnu Nish'anim Venikravim. Zacherenu Lechayim Tovim. Chonenu Bachasadeicha Harabbim. Tov Attah Lara'im Velatovim. Yemincha Peshutah Lekabel Shavim. Ki Lo Tachpotz Bemitat Chayavim. Lachen Anachnu Mashkimim Uma'arivim. Melech Mehullal Bemachanot Keruvim. Nakenu Mechete Umikol Chiyuvim. Selach Lanu Ki Fesha'einu Merubim. Anenu Lema'an Tzurim Hachatzuvim. Pitchei Teshuvah Bal Yihyu Meshullavim. Tza'akoteinu Lefaneicha Yihyu Nikravim. Karevenu Eleicha Chotzev Lehavim. Retzenu Ke'olot Parim Uchesavim. Shavnu Eleicha Ne'arim Vesavim. Temuchim Betuchim Al Rachameicha Harabbim. Rachem Terachem Aleinu Tzur Shochen Meromim. El Melech Yoshev Al Kisse Rachamim:

Hashem, God of Hosts, Who sits on the cheruvim, You have looked upon your people, return, rebellious children. Please approach me with pleasant words. Seek me and live many days. Are not Your words standing forever? Upon them, we lean and draw near. Remember us for a good life. Grace us with Your abundant kindness. You are good to the wicked and the good. Your right hand is extended to accept those who return. For You do not desire the death of the guilty. Therefore, we rise early and retire late. King, glorified in the camps of the cheruvim. Cleanse us from sin and from all obligations. Forgive us, for our transgressions are many. Answer us for the sake of the oppressed. Open paths of repentance so they will not be intertwined. May our cries be near before You. Bring us closer to You, Hewer of flames. Our desires are like burnt offerings of bulls and sheep. We have returned to You, youths and elders. Those who stumble are secure in your abundant mercy. Show mercy, have mercy upon us, Rock, dwelling on high. God, King, Who sits on the throne of mercy.

Continue with Shevet Yehudah on the next page.

Shevet Yehudah

Shevet Yehudah Bedochak	שֵׁבֶט יְהוּדָה בְּדֹחַק
Uvetza'ar. Hayish'ag Aryeh	וּבְצַעַר. הֲיִשְׁאַג אַרְיֵה
Vaya'ar: Mekavim Yeshu'atecha	בַּיַּעַר: מְקַוִּים יְשׁוּעָתְךָ
Avot Uvanim. Ha'aniyim	אָבוֹת וּבָנִים. הָעֲנִיִּים
Veha'evyonim: Amod Baperetz	וְהָאֶבְיוֹנִים: עֲמֹד בַּפֶּרֶץ
Bal Nihyeh Lischok. Lamah	בַּל נִהְיֶה לִשְׂחֹק. לָמָה
Adonai Ta'amod Berachok:	יְהֹוָה תַּעֲמֹד בְּרָחוֹק:
Yonatecha Ad Sha'arei Mavet	יוֹנָתְךָ עַד שַׁעֲרֵי מָוֶת
Higgi'ah. Yoshev Hakeruvim	הִגִּיעָה. יוֹשֵׁב הַכְּרוּבִים
Hofi'ah: Havah Lanu Ezrat	הוֹפִיעָה: הָבָה לָנוּ עֶזְרַת
Mitzar. Hayad Adonai Tiktzar:	מִצָּר. הֲיַד יְהֹוָה תִּקְצָר:
Chadesh Yameinu Vegalut	חַדֵּשׁ יָמֵינוּ בְגָלוּת
Yashan. Urah Lamah Tishan:	יָשָׁן. עוּרָה לָמָה תִישָׁן:
Zechor Baneicha Be'eretz Lo	זְכֹר בָּנֶיךָ בְּאֶרֶץ לֹא
Lahem. Vezar Lo Yikrav	לָהֶם. וְזָר לֹא יִקְרַב
Aleihem: Ketz Hanechtam	אֲלֵיהֶם: קֵץ הַנֶּחְתָּם
Galleh Legalmudah. Yismach	גַּלֵּה לְגַלְמוּדָה. יִשְׂמַח
Har Tziyon Tagelenah Venot	הַר צִיּוֹן תָּגֵלְנָה בְּנוֹת
Yehudah: Shav'atenu Ta'aleh	יְהוּדָה: שַׁוְעָתֵנוּ תַּעֲלֶה
Lishmei Meromim. El Melech	לִשְׁמֵי מְרוֹמִים. אֵל מֶלֶךְ
Yoshev Al Kisse Rachamim:	יוֹשֵׁב עַל כִּסֵּא רַחֲמִים:

The tribe of Yehudah is in distress and pain. Will the lion roar in the forest? Your salvation awaits for fathers and sons, the poor and the needy. Stand in the breach in case we become a mockery. Why, Hashem, do You stand off afar? Your dove has reached the gates of death. You who sit upon the cheruvim, appear. Bring us help from distress. Is Hashem's hand shortened? Renew our days in the old exile. Awake, why do You slumber? Remember your children in a land not theirs, and let no stranger come near them. Reveal the end of their affliction to the desolate. Let Mount Tziyon rejoice, and the daughters of Yehudah exult. Let our cries ascend to the heights of heaven, to the King Who sits on a throne of mercy.

The Thirteen Attributes of Mercy

El Melech Yoshev Al Kisse	אֵל מֶלֶךְ יוֹשֵׁב עַל כִּסֵּא
Rachamim Umitnaheg	רַחֲמִים וּמִתְנַהֵג
Bachasidut. Mochel Avonot	בַּחֲסִידוּת. מוֹחֵל עֲוֹנוֹת
Ammo Ma'avir Rishon Rishon.	עַמּוֹ מַעֲבִיר רִאשׁוֹן רִאשׁוֹן.
Marbeh Mechilah Lachata'im.	מַרְבֶּה מְחִילָה לַחַטָּאִים.
Uselichah Laposhe'im. Oseh	וּסְלִיחָה לַפּוֹשְׁעִים. עוֹשֶׂה
Tzedakot Im Kol Basar Veruach.	צְדָקוֹת עִם כָּל בָּשָׂר וְרוּחַ.
Lo Chera'atam Lahem Gomel.	לֹא כְרָעָתָם לָהֶם גּוֹמֵל.
El Horetanu Lomar Midot	אֵל הוֹרֵתָנוּ לוֹמַר מִדּוֹת
Shelosh Esreh. Zechor Lanu	שְׁלֹשׁ עֶשְׂרֵה. זְכֹר לָנוּ
Hayom Berit Shelosh Esreh.	הַיּוֹם בְּרִית שְׁלֹשׁ עֶשְׂרֵה.
Kemo Shehoda'ta Le'anav	כְּמוֹ שֶׁהוֹדַעְתָּ לֶעָנָו
Mikedem. Vechen Katuv	מִקֶּדֶם. וְכֵן כָּתוּב
Betoratach: Vayered Adonai	בְּתוֹרָתָךְ: וַיֵּרֶד יְהֹוָה
Be'anan Vayityatzev Imo Sham.	בֶּעָנָן וַיִּתְיַצֵּב עִמּוֹ שָׁם.
Vayikra Veshem, Adonai.	וַיִּקְרָא בְשֵׁם. יְהֹוָה.
Vesham Ne'emar:	וְשָׁם נֶאֱמַר:

God, King, Who sits on a throne of mercy and acts with kindness. Forgiving the sins of His people, removing them one by one. He abundantly forgives sinners and pardons transgressors. He performs acts of righteousness with all flesh and spirit. Not according to their evil deeds does He repay them. God has taught us to recite the Thirteen Attributes. Remember for us today the covenant of the Thirteen Attributes, as You made known to the humble one (Moshe) in ancient times. And so it is written in Your Torah: And Hashem descended in a cloud and stood with him there, and He called upon the name of Hashem. And there it is said,

[*] denotes a slight pause between words:

וַיַּעֲבֹר יְהוָה עַל פָּנָיו וַיִּקְרָא. יְהוָה * יְהוָה אֵל רַחוּם וְחַנּוּן. אֶרֶךְ
אַפַּיִם וְרַב חֶסֶד וֶאֱמֶת: נֹצֵר חֶסֶד לָאֲלָפִים נֹשֵׂא עָוֹן וָפֶשַׁע וְחַטָּאָה.
וְנַקֵּה: וְסָלַחְתָּ לַעֲוֹנֵנוּ וּלְחַטָּאתֵנוּ וּנְחַלְתָּנוּ:

Vaya'avor Adonai Al Panav Vayikra, Adonai | Adonai El Rachum Vechanun, Erech Apayim Verav Chesed Ve'emet: Notzer Chesed La'alafim Nose Avon Vafesha Vechata'ah, Venakeh: Vesalachta La'avonenu Ulechatatenu Unechaltanu:

And Hashem passed before him and proclaimed: "Hashem, Hashem, a God merciful and gracious, slow to anger and abounding in steadfast love and faithfulness; keeping steadfast love for thousands, forgiving iniquity, transgression, and sin, and clearing the guilty; and You will forgive our iniquities and our sins and give us our inheritance."

Rachamana

רַחֲמָנָא אִדְכַּר לָן קְיָמֵהּ דְּאַבְרָהָם רְחִימָא. בְּדִיל וַיַּעֲבֹר:

Rachamana Idkar Lan Keyameh De'avraham Rechima, Bedil Vaya'avor:

Merciful One, remember for us the merit of Avraham the loved one, on account of "And when he passed by".

רַחֲמָנָא אִדְכַר לָן קְיָמֵהּ דְּיִצְחָק עֲקֵידָא. בְּדִיל וַיַּעֲבֹר:

Rachamana Idkar Lan Keyameh Deyitzchak Akeida, Bedil Vaya'avor:

Merciful One, remember for us the merit of Yitzchak the bound one, on account of "And when he passed by".

רַחֲמָנָא אִדְכַר לָן קְיָמֵהּ דְּיַעֲקֹב שְׁלֵימָא. בְּדִיל וַיַּעֲבֹר:

Rachamana Idkar Lan Keyameh Deya'akov Sheleima, Bedil Vaya'avor:

Merciful One, remember for us the merit of Yaakov the perfect one, on account of "And when he passed by".

רַחֲמָנָא אִדְכַר לָן קְיָמֵהּ דְּמֹשֶׁה נְבִיאָה. בְּדִיל וַיַּעֲבֹר:

Rachamana Idkar Lan Keyameh Demosheh Nevi'ah, Bedil Vaya'avor:

Merciful One, remember for us the merit of Moshe the prophet, on account of "And when he passed by".

רַחֲמָנָא אִדְכַר לָן קְיָמֵהּ דְּאַהֲרֹן כַּהֲנָא. בְּדִיל וַיַּעֲבֹר:

Rachamana Idkar Lan Keyameh De'aharon Kahana, Bedil Vaya'avor:

Merciful One, remember for us the merit of Aharon the Priest, on account of "And when he passed by".

רַחֲמָנָא אִדְכַר לָן זְכוּתֵהּ דְּיוֹסֵף צַדִּיקָא. בְּדִיל וַיַּעֲבֹר:

Rachamana Idkar Lan Zechuteh Deyosef Tzaddika, Bedil Vaya'avor:

Merciful One, remember for us the merit of Yosef the righteous one, on account of "And when he passed by".

רַחֲמָנָא אִדְכַר לָן קְיָמֵהּ דְּדָוִד מַלְכָּא מְשִׁיחָא. בְּדִיל וַיַּעֲבֹר:

Rachamana Idkar Lan Keyameh Dedavid Malka Meshicha, Bedil Vaya'avor:

Merciful One, remember for us the merit of David the anointed king, on account of "And when he passed by".

רַחֲמָנָא אִדְכַּר לָן קְיָמֵהּ דְּפִינְחָס קַנָּאָה. בְּדִיל וַיַּעֲבֹר:

Rachamana Idkar Lan Keyameh Definchas Kana'ah, Bedil Vaya'avor:

Merciful One, remember for us the merit of Pinchas the zealous one, on account of "And when he passed by".

רַחֲמָנָא אִדְכַּר לָן צְלוֹתֵהּ דִּשְׁלֹמֹה מַלְכָּא. בְּדִיל וַיַּעֲבֹר:

Rachamana Idkar Lan Tzeloteh Dishlomoh Malka, Bedil Vaya'avor:

Merciful One, remember for us the prayers of King Shlomo, on account of "And when he passed by".

רַחֲמָנָא אָרֵים יְמִינָךְ וְאַצְמַח פֻּרְקָנָךְ. בְּדִיל וַיַּעֲבֹר:

Rachamana Areim Yeminach Ve'atzmach Purkanach, Bedil Vaya'avor:

Merciful One, raise Your right hand and make Your salvation sprout, on account of "And when he passed by".

רַחֲמָנָא בְּכִסּוּפֵי אַפִּין אָתֵינָא לְמִקְרֵי קַמָּךְ רַחֵם עֲלָן. בְּדִיל וַיַּעֲבֹר:

Rachamana Bechissufei Apin Ateina Lemikrei Kamach Rachem Alan, Bedil Vaya'avor:

Merciful One, we have come shamefaced to call upon Your mercy for us, on account of "And when he passed by".

רַחֲמָנָא גַּלֵּי גְבֶרְתָּךְ וּפְרֹק לָן. בְּדִיל וַיַּעֲבֹר:

Rachamana Gallei Gevurtach Uferok Lan, Bedil Vaya'avor:

Merciful One, reveal Your strength and set us free, on account of "And when he passed by".

רַחֲמָנָא דִּינָן אַפֵּיק לִנְהוֹרָא. בְּדִיל וַיַּעֲבֹר:

Rachamana Dinan Apeik Linhora, Bedil Vaya'avor:

Merciful One, bring out our judgment into light, on account of "And when he passed by".

רַחֲמָנָא דִּינָא דְחַיֵּי טָבֵי גְזֹר עֲלָן. בְּדִיל וַיַּעֲבֹר:

Rachamana Dina Dechayei Tavei Gezor Alan, Bedil Vaya'avor:
Merciful One, decree upon us a good life, on account of "And when
he passed by".

רַחֲמָנָא הַדְרָךְ שַׁוִּי עֲלָן. בְּדִיל וַיַּעֲבֹר:
Rachamana Hadrach Shavi Alan, Bedil Vaya'avor:
Merciful One, restore our fortunes, on account of "And when he
passed by".

רַחֲמָנָא וְלָא תִתְפְּרַע כְּעוֹבָדָנָא בִּישִׁין מִנָּן. בְּדִיל וַיַּעֲבֹר:
Rachamana Vela Titpera Ke'ovadana Bishin Minan, Bedil Vaya'avor:
Merciful One, do not exact retribution for our sins, on account of
"And when he passed by".

רַחֲמָנָא זִיוָךְ אַשְׁרֵי עֲלָן. בְּדִיל וַיַּעֲבֹר:
Rachamana Zivach Ashrei Alan, Bedil Vaya'avor:
Merciful One, grant us good fortune, on account of "And when he
passed by".

רַחֲמָנָא זַכְוָן חַפֵּשׂ לָן. בְּדִיל וַיַּעֲבֹר:
Rachamana Zachvan Chapes Lan, Bedil Vaya'avor:
Merciful One, find merit and set us free, on account of "And when
he passed by".

רַחֲמָנָא חֲשׁוֹב עֲלָן טַבְוָן. בְּדִיל וַיַּעֲבֹר:
Rachamana Chashov Alan Tavan, Bedil Vaya'avor:
Merciful One, consider us favorably, on account of "And when he
passed by".

רַחֲמָנָא טַבְוָן סַגִּיאָן אַיְתִי עֲלָן. בְּדִיל וַיַּעֲבֹר:
Rachamana Tavan Saggi'an Ayti Alan, Bedil Vaya'avor:
Merciful One, grant us great goodness, on account of "And when he
passed by".

רַחֲמָנָא יִתְגַּלְגְּלוּן רַחֲמָךְ עֲלָן. בְּדִיל וַיַּעֲבֹר:

Rachamana Yitgalgelun Rachamach Alan, Bedil Vaya'avor:

Merciful One, may your compassion be upon us, on account of "And when he passed by".

During the Ten Days of Repentance, add:

רַחֲמָנָא כָּתְבִינָן בְּסִפְרָא דְחַיֵּי טָבֵי. בְּדִיל וַיַּעֲבֹר:

Rachamana Katvinan Besifra Dechayei Tavei, Bedil Vaya'avor:

Merciful One, inscribe us in the Book of Good Life, on account of "And when he passed by".

רַחֲמָנָא כָּתְבִינָן בְּסִפְרָא דְרַחֲמֵי. בְּדִיל וַיַּעֲבֹר:

Rachamana Katvinan Besifra Derachamei, Bedil Vaya'avor:

Merciful One, inscribe us in the Book of Mercy, on account of "And when he passed by".

רַחֲמָנָא כָּתְבִינָן בְּסִפְרָא דְצַדִּיקֵי וַחֲסִידֵי. בְּדִיל וַיַּעֲבֹר:

Rachamana Katvinan Besifra Detzaddikei Vachasidei, Bedil Vaya'avor:

Merciful One, inscribe us in the Book of the Righteous and Pious, on account of "And when he passed by".

רַחֲמָנָא כָּתְבִינָן בְּסִפְרָא דְיִשָׁרֵי וּתְמִימֵי. בְּדִיל וַיַּעֲבֹר:

Rachamana Katvinan Besifra Disharei Utemimei, Bedil Vaya'avor:

Merciful One, inscribe us in the Book of the Upright and Perfect, on account of "And when he passed by".

רַחֲמָנָא כָּתְבִינָן בְּסִפְרָא דְפַרְנָסָתָא טַבְתָּא וּמְזוֹנֵי טָבֵי. בְּדִיל וַיַּעֲבֹר:

Rachamana Katvinan Besifra Defarnasata Tavta Umezonei Tavei, Bedil Vaya'avor:

Merciful One, inscribe us in the Book of Good Livelihood and Sustenance, on account of "And when he passed by".

רַחֲמָנָא כְּבֵשׁ חֶמְתָּא וְרָגְזָא מִנָּן. בְּדִיל וַיַּעֲבֹר:

Rachamana Kevosh Chemta Verugza Minan, Bedil Vaya'avor:

Merciful One, subdue Your anger and wrath from us, on account of
"And when he passed by".

רַחֲמָנָא לָא תַעְבֵּיד גְּמִירָא לָן. בְּדִיל וַיַּעֲבֹר:

Rachamana La Ta'beid Gemira Lan, Bedil Vaya'avor:

Merciful One, do not bring about our destruction, on account of
"And when he passed by".

רַחֲמָנָא מְחֹל וּשְׁבֹק לְחוֹבִין וְלַעֲוָיָן. בְּדִיל וַיַּעֲבֹר:

Rachamana Mechol Ushevok Lechovin Vela'avayan, Bedil
Vaya'avor:

Merciful One, forgive and release our sins and transgressions, on
account of "And when he passed by".

רַחֲמָנָא נְהוֹר טוּבָךְ אַנְהַר עֲלָן. בְּדִיל וַיַּעֲבֹר:

Rachamana Nehor Tuvach Anhar Alan, Bedil Vaya'avor:

Merciful One, let the light of Your goodness shine upon us, on
account of "And when he passed by".

רַחֲמָנָא סְעִיד וּסְמִיךְ הֱוֵי לָן. בְּדִיל וַיַּעֲבֹר:

Rachamana Se'id Usemich Hevei Lan, Bedil Vaya'avor:

Merciful One, nourish and support us, on account of "And when he
passed by".

רַחֲמָנָא עֲבֵיד עִמָּנָא אָתָא לְטַב. בְּדִיל וַיַּעֲבֹר:

Rachamana Aveid Imana Ata Letav, Bedil Vaya'avor:

Merciful One, bring us goodness, on account of "And when he
passed by".

רַחֲמָנָא פְּתַח שְׁמַיָּא לִצְלוֹתִין. בְּדִיל וַיַּעֲבֹר:

Rachamana Petach Shemaya Litzlotin, Bedil Vaya'avor:

Merciful One, open the heavens for our prayers, on account of "And when he passed by".

רַחֲמָנָא צְלוֹתָנָא קַבֵּל בְּרַעֲוָא. בְּדִיל וַיַּעֲבֹר:

Rachamana Tzelotana Kabel Bera'ava, Bedil Vaya'avor:

Merciful One, favorably accept our prayers, on account of "And when he passed by".

רַחֲמָנָא קַבֵּל צְלוֹתִין וּבָעוּתִין בְּעִדָּן עָקָתִין. בְּדִיל וַיַּעֲבֹר:

Rachamana Kabel Tzelotin Uva'utin Be'iddan Aktin, Bedil Vaya'avor:

Merciful One, accept our prayers and requests in times of difficulty, on account of "And when he passed by".

רַחֲמָנָא רַחֵם עַל נִשְׁמָתִין. בְּדִיל וַיַּעֲבֹר:

Rachamana Rachem Al Nishmatin, Bedil Vaya'avor:

Merciful One, have mercy on our souls, on account of "And when he passed by".

רַחֲמָנָא שַׁתָּא טַבְתָּא אַיְתֵי עֲלָן. בְּדִיל וַיַּעֲבֹר:

Rachamana Shatta Tavta Aytei Alan, Bedil Vaya'avor:

Merciful One, may You bring a good year upon us, on account of "And when he passed by".

רַחֲמָנָא תּוּב מֵרֻגְזָךְ. בְּדִיל וַיַּעֲבֹר:

Rachamana Tuv Merugzach, Bedil Vaya'avor:

Merciful One, subdue Your anger, on account of "And when he passed by".

רַחֲמָנָא וְלָא נֶהְדַר רֵיקָם מִן קַמָּךְ. בְּדִיל וַיַּעֲבֹר:

Rachamana Vela Nehdar Reikam Min Kamach, Bedil Vaya'avor:

Merciful One, let us not depart from Your presence empty-handed, on account of "And when he passed by".

[*] denotes a slight pause between words:

וַיַּעֲבֹר יְהֹוָה עַל פָּנָיו וַיִּקְרָא. יְהֹוָה * יְהֹוָה אֵל רַחוּם וְחַנּוּן. אֶרֶךְ
אַפַּיִם וְרַב חֶסֶד וֶאֱמֶת: נֹצֵר חֶסֶד לָאֲלָפִים נֹשֵׂא עָוֹן וָפֶשַׁע וְחַטָּאָה.
וְנַקֵּה: וְסָלַחְתָּ לַעֲוֹנֵנוּ וּלְחַטָּאתֵנוּ וּנְחַלְתָּנוּ:

Vaya'avor Adonai Al Panav Vayikra, Adonai | Adonai El Rachum
Vechanun, Erech Apayim Verav Chesed Ve'emet: Notzer Chesed
La'alafim Nose Avon Vafesha Vechata'ah, Venakeh: Vesalachta
La'avonenu Ulechatatenu Unechaltanu:

And Hashem passed by before him, and proclaimed: 'Hashem *
Hashem, God, merciful and gracious, long-suffering, and abundant
in goodness and truth; keeping mercy to the thousandth
generation, forgiving iniquity and transgression and sin, and
clearing (those who repent); and You shall forgive our iniquity and
our sin, and take us for Your inheritance.

Some congregations say the following piyut:

אָנָּא כְּעָב זְדוֹנִי תִּמְחֵהוּ. וְסָלַחְתָּ לַעֲוֹנִי כִּי רַב הוּא. וְסָלַחְתָּ לַעֲוֹנִי
כִּי רַב הוּא.

Ana Ke'av Zedoni Timchehu. Vesalachta La'avoni Ki Rav Hu.
Vesalachta La'avoni Ki Rav Hu.

Please, like a cloud, may my sin be erased. And forgive my iniquity,
for it is great. And forgive my iniquity, for it is great.

אֵיךְ יִמָּחֶה וְנִכְתַּב לְמוּל אָבִי. כִּי אֵין בְּלִבּוֹ מַחְשָׁב כְּמַחֲשָׁבִי.
לִמְחוֹת מֵאֲשֶׁר כָּתַב לְיוֹם רִיבִי. כִּי הַמִּכְתָּב מִכְתַּב אֱלֹהִים
הוּא. וְסָלַחְתָּ לַעֲוֹנִי כִּי רַב הוּא.

Eich Yimacheh Venichtav Lemul Avi. Ki Ein Belibo Machshav
Kemachashavi. Limchot Me'asher Katav Leyom Rivi. Ki Hamichtav
Michtav Elohim Hu. Vesalachta La'avoni Ki Rav Hu.

How can it be erased and written to circumcise my father. For there
is no thought in his heart like my thought. To erase what he wrote
for my dispute day. For the writing is the writing of God. And
forgive my iniquity, for it is great.

נָא אִם תַּחְקֹר וְתִדְרֹשׁ צוּר עֲלוּמָיו. אָוֶן בְּלֵילוֹ יַחֲרֹשׁ וּבְיָמָיו. וְאִם
לַחֲטָאָיו תִּדְרֹשׁ וְלַאֲשָׁמָיו. מִכַּף רֶגֶל וְעַד רֹאשׁ אָשָׁם הוּא. וְסָלַחְתָּ
לַעֲוֹנִי כִּי רַב הוּא.

Na Im Tachkor Vetidrosh Tzur Alumav. Aven Beleilo Yacharosh
Uveyamav. Ve'im Lachata'av Tidrosh Vela'ashamav. Mikaf Regel
Ve'ad Rosh Asham Hu. Vesalachta La'avoni Ki Rav Hu.

Please, if you investigate and seek the Rock of his youth. He plans
wickedness in his night and during his days. And if you seek his sins
and his guilt. From the sole of the foot to the head, he is guilty. And
forgive my iniquity, for it is great.

יֶהֶרְסוּן וְיִבְנוּן בִּי רַעְיוֹנָי. יוֹם בִּי חֲטָאַי יַעֲנוּן וּבְפָנָי. אָכֵן שְׂעִפַּי יְבִינוּן
כִּי יְהֹוָה. נֹשֵׂא עָוֹן וְחַנּוּן וְרַחוּם הוּא. וְסָלַחְתָּ לַעֲוֹנִי כִּי רַב הוּא.

Yehersun Veyivnun Bi Ra'yonai. Yom Bi Chata'ai Ya'anun
Uvefanai. Achen Se'ifai Yevinun Ki Adonai. Nose Avon Vechanun
Verachum Hu. Vesalachta La'avoni Ki Rav Hu.

My thoughts destroy and build in me. My sins torment me day and
night before me. Indeed, my lips will understand that it is Hashem.
He carries iniquity, is gracious and merciful. And forgive my iniquity,
for it is great.

מֶה לִידִידִי וּמַלְכִּי יִסָּתֵר. וְאֶשְׁפֹּךְ עֲטֶרֶת חִכִּי וְאֵין עוֹתֵר. וְאֶשְׁאַל
בְּעַד חֲלוֹם חֶשְׁכִּי וְאֵין פּוֹתֵר. וָאֹמַר לֹא אוּכַל כִּי חָתוּם
הוּא. וְסָלַחְתָּ לַעֲוֹנִי כִּי רַב הוּא.

Meh Lididi Umalki Yissater. Ve'eshpoch Ateret Chiki Ve'ein Oter.
Ve'esh'al Be'ad Chalom Cheshki Ve'ein Poter. Va'omar Lo Uchal Ki
Chatum Hu. Vesalachta La'avoni Ki Rav Hu.

What can my beloved and my king hide? And I will pour out the
supplication of my palate, and there is no advocate. And I will ask
on behalf of the dream of my darkness, and there is no interpreter.
And I said, I cannot, for it is sealed. And forgive my iniquity, for it is
great.

שׁוּבָה שִׁיבַת שְׁאֵרִית עַם הוּעַם. וּשְׁלַח מְבַשֵּׂר בִּבְרִית לְהוֹדִיעָם.

אֶת אֲשֶׁר יִהְיֶה בְּאַחֲרִית הַזַּעַם. וְנֻחַם וְאִם לֹא עַם בִּינוֹת
הוּא. וְסָלַחְתָּ לַעֲוֹנִי כִּי רַב הוּא.

Shuvah Shivat She'erit Am Hu'am. Ushelach Mevasser Bivrit
Lehodi'am. Et Asher Yihyeh Be'acharit Haza'am. Venucham Ve'im
Lo Am Binot Hu. Vesalachta La'avoni Ki Rav Hu.

Return the remainder of the startled people. And send a herald in
the covenant to inform them, what will happen at the end of the
wrath. And comfort them, even if they are not a discerning people.
And forgive my iniquity, for it is great.

הוֹסֵף יָד וְצִיר מִשְׁנֶה תַּשְׁלִיחַ. וְקֶרֶן לְנִגָּשׁ וְנַעֲנֶה תַּצְמִיחַ. יִגְבַּר וְכָל
אֲשֶׁר יַעֲשֶׂה יַצְלִיחַ. וְיִוָּדַע כִּי מָשִׁיחַ אֱלֹהִים הוּא. וְסָלַחְתָּ לַעֲוֹנִי כִּי
רַב הוּא.

Hosef Yad Vetzir Mishneh Tashliach. Vekeren Leniggas Vena'aneh
Tatzmiach. Yigbar Vechol Asher Ya'aseh Yatzliach. Veyivada Ki
Meshiach Elohim Hu. Vesalachta La'avoni Ki Rav Hu.

Add your hand and cast a double form. And grow a horn for the
oppressor, and the humble one will sprout. He will prevail and
everything he does will prosper. And it will be known that he is
God's Messiah. And forgive my iniquity, for it is great.

Anshei Emunah

Anshei Emunah Avadu. Ba'im	אַנְשֵׁי אֱמוּנָה אָבָדוּ. בָּאִים
Bechoach Ma'aseihem: Giborim	בְּכֹחַ מַעֲשֵׂיהֶם: גִּבּוֹרִים
La'amod Baperetz. Dochim Et	לַעֲמֹד בַּפֶּרֶץ. דּוֹחִים אֶת
Hagezerot: Hayu Lanu	הַגְּזֵרוֹת: הָיוּ לָנוּ
Lechomah. Ulemachseh Beyom	לְחוֹמָה. וּלְמַחְסֶה בְּיוֹם
Za'am: Zo'achim Af	זַעַם: זוֹעֲכִים אַף
Belachasham. Chemah Atzeru	בְּלַחֲשָׁם. חֵמָה עָצְרוּ
Beshave'am: Terem Kera'ucha	בְּשַׁוְּעָם: טֶרֶם קְרָאוּךְ
Anitam. Yode'im La'ator	עֲנִיתָם. יוֹדְעִים לַעֲתֹר

Uleratzot: Ke'av Richamta	וּלְרַצּוֹת: כְּאָב רִחַמְתָּ
Lema'anam. Lo Heshivota	לְמַעֲנָם. לֹא הֱשִׁיבוֹתָ
Peneihem Reikam: Merov	פְּנֵיהֶם רֵיקָם: מֵרֹב
Avoneinu Avadnum. Ne'esfu	עֲוֹנֵינוּ אֲבַדְנוּם. נֶאֶסְפוּ
Menu Bachata'einu: Sa'u Hemah	מֵנּוּ בַּחֲטָאֵינוּ: סָעוּ הֵמָּה
Limnuchot. Azevu Otanu	לִמְנוּחוֹת. עָזְבוּ אוֹתָנוּ
La'anachot: Passu Goderei	לַאֲנָחוֹת: פַּסּוּ גוֹדְרֵי
Gader. Tzumetu Meshivei	גָדֵר. צֻמְּתוּ מְשִׁיבֵי
Chemah: Kamim Baperetz Ayin.	חֵמָה: קָמִים בַּפֶּרֶץ אָיִן.
Re'uyim Leratzotecha Afesu:	רְאוּיִים לְרַצּוֹתְךָ אָפֵסוּ:
Shotatnu Be'arba Pinot. Terufah	שׁוֹטַטְנוּ בְּאַרְבַּע פִּנּוֹת. תְּרוּפָה
Lo Matzanu: Shavnu Eleicha	לֹא מָצָאנוּ: שַׁבְנוּ אֵלֶיךָ
Bevoshet Paneinu. Leshacharach	בְּבֹשֶׁת פָּנֵינוּ. לְשַׁחֲרָךְ
El Be'et Tzaroteinu:	אֵל בְּעֵת צָרוֹתֵינוּ:

Men of faith were lost; they come with the strength of their deeds:
mighty ones to stand in the breach. They pushed back the decrees;
they were a wall and a refuge for us in the day of wrath. They
subdued anger with their whispers; they subdued wrath with their
cries. Before they called You, You answered them. They knew how
to plead and to satisfy. Like a father, You showed mercy for their
sake. You did not turn away their faces empty-handed; because of
our many iniquities, we lost them. They were gathered from us
because of our sins; they went to their resting places and they left us
to anguish. There are none to protect the fence. The restrainers of
wrath are diminished; those who rise in the breach are no more.
The worthy of pleasing You have ceased. We wander in the four
corners [of the earth]. We have not found a remedy. We return to
You with shame on our faces. To You, God, at the time of our
troubles.

The Thirteen Attributes of Mercy

El Melech Yoshev Al Kisse	אֵל מֶלֶךְ יוֹשֵׁב עַל כִּסֵּא
Rachamim Umitnaheg	רַחֲמִים וּמִתְנַהֵג
Bachasidut. Mochel Avonot	בַּחֲסִידוּת. מוֹחֵל עֲוֹנוֹת
Ammo Ma'avir Rishon Rishon.	עַמּוֹ מַעֲבִיר רִאשׁוֹן רִאשׁוֹן.
Marbeh Mechilah Lachata'im.	מַרְבֶּה מְחִילָה לַחַטָּאִים.
Uselichah Laposhe'im. Oseh	וּסְלִיחָה לַפּוֹשְׁעִים. עוֹשֶׂה
Tzedakot Im Kol Basar Veruach.	צְדָקוֹת עִם כָּל בָּשָׂר וְרוּחַ.
Lo Chera'atam Lahem Gomel.	לֹא כְרָעָתָם לָהֶם גּוֹמֵל.
El Horetanu Lomar Midot	אֵל הוֹרֵתָנוּ לוֹמַר מִדּוֹת
Shelosh Esreh. Zechor Lanu	שְׁלֹשׁ עֶשְׂרֵה. זְכֹר לָנוּ
Hayom Berit Shelosh Esreh.	הַיּוֹם בְּרִית שְׁלֹשׁ עֶשְׂרֵה.
Kemo Shehoda'ta Le'anav	כְּמוֹ שֶׁהוֹדַעְתָּ לֶעָנָו
Mikedem. Vechen Katuv	מִקֶּדֶם. וְכֵן כָּתוּב
Betoratach: Vayered Adonai	בְּתוֹרָתָךְ: וַיֵּרֶד יְהֹוָה
Be'anan Vayityatzev Imo Sham.	בֶּעָנָן וַיִּתְיַצֵּב עִמּוֹ שָׁם.
Vayikra Veshem, Adonai.	וַיִּקְרָא בְשֵׁם. יְהֹוָה.
Vesham Ne'emar:	וְשָׁם נֶאֱמַר:

God, King, Who sits on a throne of mercy and acts with kindness. Forgiving the sins of His people, removing them one by one. He abundantly forgives sinners and pardons transgressors. He performs acts of righteousness with all flesh and spirit. Not according to their evil deeds does He repay them. God has taught us to recite the Thirteen Attributes. Remember for us today the covenant of the Thirteen Attributes, as You made known to the humble one (Moshe) in ancient times. And so it is written in Your Torah: And Hashem descended in a cloud and stood with him there, and He called upon the name of Hashem. And there it is said,

[*] denotes a slight pause between words:

וַיַּעֲבֹר יְהֹוָה עַל פָּנָיו וַיִּקְרָא. יְהֹוָה * יְהֹוָה אֵל רַחוּם וְחַנּוּן. אֶרֶךְ
אַפַּיִם וְרַב חֶסֶד וֶאֱמֶת: נֹצֵר חֶסֶד לָאֲלָפִים נֹשֵׂא עָוֹן וָפֶשַׁע וְחַטָּאָה.
וְנַקֵּה: וְסָלַחְתָּ לַעֲוֹנֵנוּ וּלְחַטָּאתֵנוּ וּנְחַלְתָּנוּ:

Vaya'avor Adonai Al Panav Vayikra, Adonai | Adonai El Rachum
Vechanun, Erech Apayim Verav Chesed Ve'emet: Notzer Chesed
La'alafim Nose Avon Vafesha Vechata'ah, Venakeh: Vesalachta
La'avonenu Ulechatatenu Unechaltanu:

And Hashem passed by before him, and proclaimed: 'Hashem *
Hashem, God, merciful and gracious, long-suffering, and abundant
in goodness and truth; keeping mercy to the thousandth
generation, forgiving iniquity and transgression and sin, and
clearing (those who repent); and You shall forgive our iniquity and
our sin, and take us for Your inheritance.

Tamahnu Mera'ot

Tamahnu Mera'ot. Tashash	תָּמַהְנוּ מֵרָעוֹת. תָּשַׁשׁ
Kochenu Mitzarot: Shachnu Ad	כֹּחֵנוּ מִצָּרוֹת: שַׁחְנוּ עַד
Lim'od. Shafalnu Ad Afar:	לִמְאֹד. שָׁפַלְנוּ עַד עָפָר:
Rachum Kach Hi Midatenu.	רַחוּם כָּךְ הִיא מִדָּתֵנוּ.
Keshei Oref Umamrim Anachnu:	קְשֵׁי עֹרֶף וּמַמְרִים אֲנַחְנוּ:
Tza'aknu Befinu Chatanu.	צָעַקְנוּ בְּפִינוּ חָטָאנוּ.
Petaltol Ve'ikesh Libenu: Elyon	פְּתַלְתֹּל וְעִקֵּשׁ לִבֵּנוּ: עֶלְיוֹן
Rachameicha Me'olam. Selichah	רַחֲמֶיךָ מֵעוֹלָם. סְלִיחָה
Imecha Hi: Nicham Al Hara'ah.	עִמְּךָ הִיא: נִחַם עַל הָרָעָה.
Matteh Chelapei Chesed: Lo	מַטֶּה כְּלַפֵּי חֶסֶד: לֹא
Tit'allam Be'itot Ka'el. Ki	תִתְעַלָּם בְּעִתּוֹת כָּאֵל. כִּי
Vetzarah Gedolah Anachnu:	בְצָרָה גְדוֹלָה אֲנַחְנוּ:

Yivada Le'einei Hakol. Tuvecha	יֵדַע לְעֵינֵי הַכֹּל. טוּבְךָ
Vechasdecha Imanu: Chatom	וְחַסְדְּךָ עִמָּנוּ: חֲתֹם
Peh Satan Ve'al Yastin Aleinu.	פֶּה שָׂטָן וְאַל יַשְׂטִין עָלֵינוּ.
Ze'om Bo Veyiddom: Veya'amod	זְעָם בּוֹ וְיִדֹּם: וְיַעֲמֹד
Melitz Tov Letzaddekenu. Hu	מֵלִיץ טוֹב לְצַדְּקֵנוּ. הוּא
Yaggid Yasherenu: Deracheicha	יַגִּיד יָשְׁרֵנוּ: דְּרָכֶיךָ
Rachum Vechanun. Gillita	רַחוּם וְחַנּוּן. גִּלִּיתָ
Lene'eman Bayit: Bevaksho Az	לְנֶאֱמָן בַּיִת: בְּבַקְשׁוֹ אָז
Millefaneicha. Emunatecha	מִלְּפָנֶיךָ. אֱמוּנָתְךָ
Hoda'ta Lo:	הוֹדַעְתָּ לוֹ:

Stunned by our woes. Weakened by sorrows, we are brought very low and are humbled to the dust. Merciful One, we may be stiff-necked and rebellious, Such is our nature; Our mouths may declare "we have sinned," Our hearts are hard and perverse, yet You, Supremely Exalted, are merciful from old, And pardon is always with You. Repenting of evil and inclining to mercy, do not hide Yourself in times like these, for we are sorely troubled. Make known to all that Your goodness and love are still with us. Seal the mouth of the accuser that he cannot indict us; Rebuke him that is silent. Let a good spokesman arise to declare our uprightness and absolve us. Merciful, gracious God, to Moshe, faithful in all Your House, You have revealed Your ways at his request to You, And You made him know Your truth.

The Thirteen Attributes of Mercy

אֵל מֶלֶךְ יוֹשֵׁב עַל כִּסֵּא רַחֲמִים וּמִתְנַהֵג בַּחֲסִידוּת. מוֹחֵל עֲוֹנוֹת עַמּוֹ מַעֲבִיר רִאשׁוֹן רִאשׁוֹן. מַרְבֶּה מְחִילָה לַחַטָּאִים. וּסְלִיחָה לַפּוֹשְׁעִים. עוֹשֶׂה צְדָקוֹת עִם כָּל בָּשָׂר וְרוּחַ. לֹא כְרָעָתָם לָהֶם גוֹמֵל. אֵל הוֹרֵתָנוּ לוֹמַר מִדּוֹת שְׁלֹשׁ עֶשְׂרֵה. זְכֹר לָנוּ הַיּוֹם בְּרִית

שָׁלֹשׁ עֶשְׂרֵה. כְּמוֹ שֶׁהוֹדַעְתָּ לֶעָנָו מִקֶּדֶם. וְכֵן כָּתוּב בְּתוֹרָתֶךָ. וַיֵּרֶד יְהֹוָה בֶּעָנָן וַיִּתְיַצֵּב עִמּוֹ שָׁם. וַיִּקְרָא בְשֵׁם. יְהֹוָה. וְשָׁם נֶאֱמַר:

El Melech Yoshev Al Kisse Rachamim Umitnaheg Bachasidut. Mochel Avonot Ammo Ma'avir Rishon Rishon. Marbeh Mechilah Lachata'im. Uselichah Laposhe'im. Oseh Tzedakot Im Kol Basar Veruach. Lo Chera'atam Lahem Gomel. El Horetanu Lomar Midot Shelosh Esreh. Zechor Lanu Hayom Berit Shelosh Esreh. Kemo Shehoda'ta Le'anav Mikedem. Vechen Katuv Betoratach. Vayered Adonai Be'anan Vayityatzev Imo Sham. Vayikra Veshem, Adonai. Vesham Ne'emar:

Sovereign God, enthroned in mercy, You deal with us tenderly, again pardoning the sins of Your people even though they sin again. You are ever ready to give pardon to sinners and forgiveness to transgressors, acting in charity towards all with breath of life, not requiting them according to the evil they do. You, God, Who has taught us to repeat the thirteen attributes of mercy, remember to us this day the covenant of those attributes, as You revealed them of old to Moshe the humble, in the words written in Your Torah: "And Hashem descended in the cloud, and stood with him there, and proclaimed the name of Hashem." (Exodus 34:5) And there it says:

[*] denotes a slight pause between words:

וַיַּעֲבֹר יְהֹוָה עַל פָּנָיו וַיִּקְרָא. יְהֹוָה * יְהֹוָה אֵל רַחוּם וְחַנּוּן. אֶרֶךְ אַפַּיִם וְרַב חֶסֶד וֶאֱמֶת: נֹצֵר חֶסֶד לָאֲלָפִים נֹשֵׂא עָוֹן וָפֶשַׁע וְחַטָּאָה. וְנַקֵּה: וְסָלַחְתָּ לַעֲוֹנֵנוּ וּלְחַטָּאתֵנוּ וּנְחַלְתָּנוּ:

Vaya'avor Adonai Al Panav Vayikra, Adonai | Adonai El Rachum Vechanun, Erech Apayim Verav Chesed Ve'emet: Notzer Chesed La'alafim Nose Avon Vafesha Vechata'ah, Venakeh: Vesalachta La'avonenu Ulechatatenu Unechaltanu:

And Hashem passed by before him, and proclaimed: 'Hashem * Hashem, God, merciful and gracious, long-suffering, and abundant in goodness and truth; keeping mercy to the thousandth generation, forgiving iniquity and transgression and sin, and clearing (those who repent); and You shall forgive our iniquity and our sin, and take us for Your inheritance.

Al Ta'as

Eloheinu Velohei Avoteinu. Al	אֱלֹהֵינוּ וֵאלֹהֵי אֲבוֹתֵינוּ. אַל
Ta'as Imanu Chalah. Tochez	תַּעַשׂ עִמָּנוּ כָלָה. תֹּאחֵז
Yadecha Bamishpat: Bevo	יָדְךָ בַּמִּשְׁפָּט: בְּבֹא
Tochechah Negdecha. Shemenu	תוֹכֵחָה נֶגְדֶּךָ. שְׁמֵנוּ
Misifrecha Al Temach:	מִסִּפְרְךָ אַל תֶּמַח:
Gishtecha Lachakor Musar.	גִּשְׁתְּךָ לַחֲקֹר מוּסָר.
Rachameicha Yekaddemu	רַחֲמֶיךָ יְקַדְּמוּ
Rogzecha: Dallut Ma'asim	רָגְזֶךָ: דַּלּוּת מַעֲשִׂים
Beshurecha. Karev Tzedek	בְּשׁוּרֶךָ. קָרֵב צֶדֶק
Me'eleicha: Horenu,	מֵאֵלֶיךָ: הוֹרֵנוּ.
Beza'akenu Lach. Tzav	בְּזַעֲקֵנוּ לָךְ. צַו
Yeshu'atenu Bemafgia': Vetashiv	יְשׁוּעָתֵנוּ בְּמַפְגִּיעַ: וְתָשִׁיב
Shevut Oholei Tam. Petachav	שְׁבוּת אָהֳלֵי תָם. פְּתָחָיו
Re'eh Ki Shamemu: Zechor	רְאֵה כִּי שָׁמֵמוּ: זְכֹר
Na'amta. Edut Lo Tishachach	נָאַמְתָּ. עֵדוּת לֹא תִשָּׁכַח
Mipi Zar'o: Chotam Te'udah	מִפִּי זַרְעוֹ: חוֹתָם תְּעוּדָה
Tattir. Sodecha Sim	תַּתִּיר. סוֹדְךָ שִׂים
Belimudecha. Tabur Aggan	בְּלִמּוּדֶךָ. טַבּוּר אַגַּן
Hassahar. Na Al Yechsar	הַסַּהַר. נָא אַל יֶחְסַר
Hamazeg: Yah, Da Et Yisra'el	הַמָּזֶג: יָהּ. דַּע אֶת יִשְׂרָאֵל
Asher Yeda'ucha. Magger Et	אֲשֶׁר יְדָעוּךָ. מַגֵּר אֶת
Hagoyim Asher Lo Yeda'ucha:	הַגּוֹיִם אֲשֶׁר לֹא יְדָעוּךָ:
Ki Tashiv Levitzaron. Lechudim	כִּי תָשִׁיב לְבִצָּרוֹן. לְכוּדִים
Asirei Hattikvah:	אֲסִירֵי הַתִּקְוָה:

Our God and the God of our fathers. Do not utterly destroy us.
Hold Your hand in judgment. When rebuke [against us] comes

before You, do not erase us from your book. As You approach to examine for discipline, let Your mercy come before Your anger. As You observe the poverty of our deeds, bring near righteousness from You. Teach us as we cry out to You. Command our salvation by intervention. And return the captives of the innocent one [Yaakov]. See that their entrances are desolate. Remember Your promise: the testimony will not be forgotten from the mouth of his offspring. Remove the seal from upon the testimony [Torah]. Place your secret in your students [Yisrael]. The center of the world [the Sanhedrin], please may they never lack mixture [instruction]; Hashem, know Yisrael who knows You. Drive away the nations who do not know You. For You will return to the fortress [Yerushalayim], the captives of hope who cling [to God]:

Ribbono Shel Olam

Ribbono Shel Olam. Etvadeh Al	רִבּוֹנוֹ שֶׁל עוֹלָם. אֶתְוַדֶּה עַל
Averot. Kallot Vachamurot.	עֲבֵרוֹת. קַלּוֹת וַחֲמוּרוֹת.
Balaylah Lesof Ashmurot: Yitzri	בַּלַּיְלָה לְסוֹף אַשְׁמוּרוֹת: יִצְרִי
Alilot Beresha Lehit'olel. Shomer	עֲלִילוֹת בְּרֶשַׁע לְהִתְעוֹלֵל. שׁוֹמֵר
Mah Milaylah Shomer Mah	מַה מִלַּיְלָה שׁוֹמֵר מַה
Milleil: Libi Ve'einai Lachato	מִלֵּיל: לִבִּי וְעֵינַי לַחֲטֹא
Ye'otu. Veyom Valaylah Lo	יֵאוֹתוּ. וְיוֹם וָלַיְלָה לֹא
Yishbotu: Ushe'ar Evarai La'asot	יִשְׁבֹּתוּ: וּשְׁאָר אֵבָרַי לַעֲשׂוֹת
Hara Be'eineicha Yitlachashu.	הָרַע בְּעֵינֶיךָ יִתְלַחֲשׁוּ.
Kol Hayom Vechol Halaylah	כָּל הַיּוֹם וְכָל הַלַּיְלָה
Tamid Lo Yecheshu: Veya'an	תָּמִיד לֹא יֶחֱשׁוּ: וְיַעַן
Asher Avarti Al Mitzvot Aseh	אֲשֶׁר עָבַרְתִּי עַל מִצְוֹת עֲשֵׂה
Ve'al Mitzvot Lo Ta'aseh. Mi	וְעַל מִצְוֹת לֹא תַעֲשֶׂה. מִי

Yiten Ve'ascheh Bechol Layelah	יִתֵּן וְאֶשְׁחֶה בְּכָל לַיְלָה
Mitati Bedim'ati Arsi Amseh:	מִטָּתִי בְּדִמְעָתִי עַרְשִׂי אַמְסֶה:
Ulai Yishma Kol Bichyi Nora	אוּלַי יִשְׁמַע קוֹל בִּכְיִי נוֹרָא
Alilah. Yom Tza'akti Ballayelah:	עֲלִילָה. יוֹם צָעַקְתִּי בַּלָּיְלָה:
Ekra Yomam Ve'arim Koli. Al	אֶקְרָא יוֹמָם וְאָרִים קוֹלִי. עַל
Pish'i Uma'ali. Velayelah Velo	פִּשְׁעִי וּמַעֲלִי. וְלַיְלָה וְלֹא
Dumiyah Li: Et Miktzat Chata'ai	דוּמִיָּה לִי: אֶת מִקְצַת חֲטָאַי
Ani Mazkir Lifnei Tzofeh Atidot.	אֲנִי מַזְכִּיר לִפְנֵי צוֹפֶה עֲתִידוֹת.
Layelah Akum Lehodot: Ve'odeh	לַיְלָה אָקוּם לְהוֹדוֹת: וְאוֹדֶה
Alei Fesha'ai Uzedonai.	עֲלֵי פְּשָׁעַי וּזְדוֹנַי.
Halaylah Hazeh l'Adonai:	הַלַּיְלָה הַזֶּה לַיהוָה:

Master of the universe. I will confess my transgressions, minor and severe. At night, at the end of the watches, my inclination plots wickedness to act frivolously. Guardian, what will be of the night? Guardian, what will be of the night? My heart and my eyes desire to sin. And day and night they do not rest. And the rest of my limbs to do evil in your eyes, they whisper. All day and all night, they never cease. And because I have transgressed both positive commandments and negative commandments, I soak every night my bed with my tears, my bed I dissolve. Perhaps the voice of my weeping at night will be heard by He Who does awesome miracles, on the day I cry out at night. I call out by day and lift up my voice over my sin and my trespass. And the night is not silent for me. I mention some of my sins before the One Who watches the future. At night I rise to confess: and I will confess my sins and my willful transgressions. This night is to Hashem:

Continue on the next page with Ana Adonai.

Ana Adonai

Ana Adonai Eloheinu Velohei	אָנָּא יְהֹוָה אֱלֹהֵינוּ וֵאלֹהֵי
Avoteinu. Tavo Lefaneicha	אֲבוֹתֵינוּ. תָּבֹא לְפָנֶיךָ
Tefillatenu. Ve'al Tit'allam	תְּפִלָּתֵנוּ. וְאַל תִּתְעַלַּם
Malkenu Mitechinatenu. She'ein	מַלְכֵּנוּ מִתְּחִנָּתֵנוּ. שֶׁאֵין
Anachnu Azei Fanim Ukeshei	אֲנַחְנוּ עַזֵּי פָנִים וּקְשֵׁי
Oref Lomar Lefaneicha Adonai	עֹרֶף לוֹמַר לְפָנֶיךָ יְהֹוָה
Eloheinu Velohei Avoteinu,	אֱלֹהֵינוּ וֵאלֹהֵי אֲבוֹתֵינוּ.
Tzaddikim Anachnu Velo	צַדִּיקִים אֲנַחְנוּ וְלֹא
Chatanu. Aval Chatanu. Avinu.	חָטָאנוּ. אֲבָל חָטָאנוּ. עָוִינוּ.
Pasha'nu. Anachnu Va'avoteinu	פָּשַׁעְנוּ. אֲנַחְנוּ וַאֲבוֹתֵינוּ
Ve'anshei Veitenu:	וְאַנְשֵׁי בֵיתֵנוּ:

Please, Hashem our God and God of our fathers. Let our prayer come before You. And do not hide, our King, from our supplication. For we are not brazen-faced and stiff-necked to say before you, Hashem our God and God of our fathers, we are righteous and have not sinned. But we have sinned. We have been iniquitous. We have transgressed. We and our fathers and the people of our house:

Chatati Odi'acha

Chatati Odi'acha Va'avoni Lo	חַטָאתִי אוֹדִיעֲךָ וַעֲוֹנִי לֹא
Chissiti. Amarti Odeh Alei	כִסִּיתִי. אָמַרְתִּי אוֹדֶה עֲלֵי
Fesha'ai L'Adonai. Ve'attah	פְשָׁעַי לַיהֹוָה. וְאַתָּה
Nasata Avon Chatati Selah:	נָשָׂאתָ עֲוֹן חַטָאתִי סֶלָה:
(Mechasseh Fesha'av Lo	(מְכַסֶּה פְשָׁעָיו לֹא
Yatzliach. Umodeh Ve'ozev	יַצְלִיחַ. וּמוֹדֶה וְעֹזֵב
Yerucham:)	יְרֻחָם:)

I have sinned, I acknowledge You and do not hide my iniquity. I said, I will confess my transgressions to Hashem. And You forgave the iniquity of my sin. Selah. (And it is said, Whoever conceals his transgressions will not prosper, but he who confesses and forsakes them will find mercy.)

Ashamnu

Ashamnu. Achalnu Ma'achalot	אָשַׁמְנוּ. אָכַלְנוּ מַאֲכָלוֹת
Asurot. Bagadnu. Bitalnu	אֲסוּרוֹת. בָּגַדְנוּ. בִּטַּלְנוּ
Toratecha. Gazalnu. Ganavnu.	תוֹרָתֶךָ. גָּזַלְנוּ. גָּנַבְנוּ.
Ga'inu. Dibarnu Dofi Velashon	גָּאִינוּ. דִּבַּרְנוּ דֹפִי וְלָשׁוֹן
Hara. Dibarnu Echad Bapeh	הָרָע. דִּבַּרְנוּ אֶחָד בַּפֶּה
Ve'echad Ballev. He'evinu.	וְאֶחָד בַּלֵּב. הֶעֱוִינוּ.
Hirharnu Hirhurim Ra'im Bayom	הִרְהַרְנוּ הִרְהוּרִים רָעִים בַּיוֹם
Uvanu Lidei Tum'at Keri	וּבָאנוּ לִידֵי טֻמְאַת קֶרִי
Balaylah. Vehirsha'nu. Vi'adnu	בַּלַּיְלָה. וְהִרְשַׁעְנוּ. וְיָעַדְנוּ
Atzmenu Lidvar Averah. Zadnu.	עַצְמֵנוּ לִדְבַר עֲבֵרָה. זַדְנוּ.
Zaninu Achar Libenu Ve'eineinu.	זָנִינוּ אַחַר לִבֵּנוּ וְעֵינֵינוּ.
Chamasnu. Chamadnu. Tafalnu	חָמַסְנוּ. חָמַדְנוּ. טָפַלְנוּ
Sheker Umirmah. Ya'atznu Etzot	שֶׁקֶר וּמִרְמָה. יָעַצְנוּ עֵצוֹת
Ra'ot Ad Ein Cheker. Kizavnu.	רָעוֹת עַד אֵין חֵקֶר. כִּזַּבְנוּ.
Ka'asnu. Latznu. Lotzatznu.	כָּעַסְנוּ. לַצְנוּ. לוֹצַצְנוּ.
Maradnu. Marinu Devareicha.	מָרַדְנוּ. מָרִינוּ דְבָרֶיךָ.
Maradnu Vemalchut Shamayim.	מָרַדְנוּ בְּמַלְכוּת שָׁמַיִם.
Maradnu Vemalchut Beit David.	מָרַדְנוּ בְּמַלְכוּת בֵּית דָּוִד.
Ma'asnu Veveit Hamikdash,	מָאַסְנוּ בְּבֵית הַמִּקְדָּשׁ.
Ushelashetam Anachnu	וּשְׁלָשְׁתָּם אֲנַחְנוּ

Mevakshim. Ni'atznu. Ni'afnu.	מְבַקְשִׁים. נִאַצְנוּ. נִאַפְנוּ.
Nishba'nu Lashave Velasheker.	נִשְׁבַּעְנוּ לַשָּׁוְא וְלַשֶּׁקֶר.
Nadarnu Velo Shillamnu.	נָדַרְנוּ וְלֹא שִׁלַּמְנוּ.
Sararnu. Sorerim Umorim	סָרַרְנוּ. סוֹרְרִים וּמוֹרִים
Hayinu. Avinu. Avarnu Al	הָיִינוּ. עָוִינוּ. עָבַרְנוּ עַל
Mitzvot Aseh Ve'al Mitzvot Lo	מִצְוֹת עֲשֵׂה וְעַל מִצְוֹת לֹא
Ta'aseh. Avarnu Al Keritot	תַעֲשֶׂה. עָבַרְנוּ עַל כְּרִיתוֹת
Umitot Beit Din. Avarnu Al	וּמִיתוֹת בֵּית דִּין. עָבַרְנוּ עַל
Chillul Hashem. Pasha'nu.	חִלוּל הַשֵּׁם. פָּשַׁעְנוּ.
Pagamnu Be'ot Berit Kodesh.	פָּגַמְנוּ בְּאוֹת בְּרִית קֹדֶשׁ.
Tzararnu. Tzi'arnu Av Va'em.	צָרַרְנוּ. צִעַרְנוּ אָב וָאֵם.
Kishinu Oref. Kilkalnu Tzinorot	קָשִׁינוּ עֹרֶף. קִלְקַלְנוּ צִנּוֹרוֹת
Hashefa. Rasha'nu. Ra'im	הַשֶּׁפַע. רָשַׁעְנוּ. רָעִים
Lashamayim Velaberiyot Hayinu.	לַשָּׁמַיִם וְלַבְּרִיּוֹת הָיִינוּ.
Shichatnu. Shikarnu. Shichatnu	שִׁחַתְנוּ. שִׁקַּרְנוּ. שִׁחַתְנוּ
Zera Kodesh Levattalah Uvaranu	זֶרַע קֹדֶשׁ לְבַטָּלָה וּבָרָאנוּ
Mashchit Lechabel. (Gam	מַשְׁחִית לְחַבֵּל. (גַם
Bichnafeinu Nimtze'u Dam Nafshot	בִּכְנָפֵינוּ נִמְצְאוּ דַם נַפְשׁוֹת
Evyonim Nekiyim Vehineh Dim'at	אֶבְיוֹנִים נְקִיִּים וְהִנֵּה דִּמְעַת
Ha'ashukim Ve'ein Lahem Menachem.	הָעֲשׁוּקִים וְאֵין לָהֶם מְנַחֵם.
Libi Libi Al Challeihem. Me'ai Me'ai Al	לִבִּי לִבִּי עַל חַלְלֵיהֶם. מֵעַי מֵעַי עַל
Harugeihem. Oy Lerasha Ra, Ki Gemul	הֲרוּגֵיהֶם. אוֹי לְרָשָׁע רָע. כִּי גְמוּל
Yadav Ye'aseh Lo.) Ti'avnu. Ta'inu	יָדָיו יֵעָשֶׂה לוֹ.) תִּעַבְנוּ. תָּעִינוּ
Veti'ata'nu. Vesarnu	וְתִעֲתַעְנוּ. וְסַרְנוּ
Mimitzvoteicha	מִמִּצְוֹתֶיךָ
Umimishpateicha Hatovim Velo	וּמִמִּשְׁפָּטֶיךָ הַטּוֹבִים וְלֹא
Shavah Lanu. Ve'attah Tzaddik Al	שָׁוָה לָנוּ. וְאַתָּה צַדִּיק עַל

Kol Habba Aleinu. Ki Emet Asita.   כָּל הַבָּא עָלֵינוּ. כִּי אֱמֶת עָשִׂיתָ.

Va'anachnu Hirsha'enu: וַאֲנַחְנוּ הִרְשָׁעְנוּ:

We have been guilty, we have eaten forbidden foods, we have betrayed, we have neglected Your Torah, we have stolen, we have robbed, we have been arrogant, we have spoken deceit and slander, we have spoken with double intentions, we have acted perversely, we have entertained wicked thoughts during the day and have been led to impurity at night, we have been wicked, we have made ourselves commit sin. We have acted presumptuously, we have lusted after our hearts and eyes, we have extorted, we have coveted, we have dealt falsely and deceitfully, we have given bad advise beyond measure, we have lied, we have been angry, we have mocked, we have derided, we have rebelled, we have rebelled against Your words, we have rebelled against the kingdom of Heaven, we have rebelled against the kingdom of the house of David, we have despised the Temple, and yet we seek the three of them. We have enraged, we have committed adultery, we have sworn falsely and deceitfully, we have vowed and have not fulfilled, we have strayed, we have been rebellious and disobedient, we have sinned, we have transgressed the positive commandments and prohibitions, we have transgressed the commandments that carry punishments of Karet and death executed by the court, we have transgressed the desecration of the Name (Hashem). We have trespassed, we have defiled the holy covenant, we have oppressed, we have grieved father and mother, we have been stiff-necked, we have disrupted the channels of abundance, we have been wicked, we have been evil to Heaven and to Creation. We have corrupted, we have lied, we have wasted the holy seed in vain and created destruction to harm, (Even on our corners we have found the blood of innocent, poor souls and behold the tears of the oppressed with no comfort. My heart, my heart for their ruin. My bowels, my bowels for their slaughter. Woe to the wicked, for the reward of his hands will be done to him.) We have abhorred, we have erred and gone astray, we have turned away from Your commandments and Your good judgments, and it has been of no benefit to us. And You are righteous in all that has come upon us. For You have acted in truth, and we have been wicked.

Ashamnu Mikol Am

Ashamnu Mikol Am. Boshenu	אָשַׁמְנוּ מִכָּל עָם. בּוֹשְׁנוּ
Mikol Goy. Galah Mimenu	מִכָּל גּוֹי. גָּלָה מִמֶּנוּ
Masos. Daveh Libenu	מָשׂוֹשׂ. דָּוֶה לִבֵּנוּ
Bachata'einu. Hachebal Evyenu.	בַּחֲטָאֵינוּ. הָחֻבַּל אֶוְיֵנוּ.
Venifra Pe'erenu. Zevul	וְנִפְרַע פְּאֵרֵנוּ. זְבוּל
Mikdashenu. Charev	מִקְדָּשֵׁנוּ. חָרֵב
Ba'avoneinu. Tiratenu Hayetah	בַּעֲוֹנֵינוּ. טִירָתֵנוּ הָיְתָה
Leshamah. Yefi Admatenu	לְשַׁמָּה. יְפִי אַדְמָתֵנוּ
Lezarim. Kochenu Lenacherim:	לְזָרִים. כֹּחֵנוּ לְנָכְרִים:
Le'eineinu Asheku Amalenu.	לְעֵינֵינוּ עָשְׁקוּ עֲמָלֵנוּ.
Memushach Umorat Mimenu.	מְמֻשָּׁךְ וּמֹרָט מִמֶּנוּ.
Natenu Ullam Aleinu. Savalnu	נָתְנוּ עֻלָּם עָלֵינוּ. סָבַלְנוּ
Al Shichmenu. Avadim Mashelu	עַל שִׁכְמֵנוּ. עֲבָדִים מָשְׁלוּ
Vanu. Porek Ein Miyadam.	בָנוּ. פֹּרֵק אֵין מִיָּדָם.
Tzarot Rabbot Sevavunu.	צָרוֹת רַבּוֹת סְבָבוּנוּ.
Keranucha Adonai Eloheinu.	קְרָאנוּךְ יְהוָה אֱלֹהֵינוּ.
Richakta Mimenu Ba'avoneinu.	רִחַקְתָּ מִמֶּנוּ בַּעֲוֹנֵינוּ.
Shavnu Me'achareicha. Ta'inu	שַׁבְנוּ מֵאַחֲרֶיךָ. תָּעִינוּ
Katzon Ve'avadnu. Va'adayin Lo	כַּצֹּאן וְאָבַדְנוּ. וַעֲדַיִן לֹא
Shavnu Mite'iyatenu.	שַׁבְנוּ מִתְּעִיָּתֵנוּ.

We have been guilty more than any other people. We have been shamed more than any nation. Joy has been exiled from us. Our hearts are sick because of our sins. Our Beit HaMikdash has been destroyed. Our strength has failed. Our glory has been taken away. Our Temple has been destroyed because of our iniquity. Our city has become a desolation. The beauty of our land has been given to strangers. Our strength has gone to foreigners. Before our eyes, they have oppressed our labor. It is dragged away and cut off from us. They have put their yoke upon us. We have borne it on our shoulders. Slaves have ruled over us. There is no one to deliver us from their hand. Many troubles have surrounded us. We have called upon You, Hashem our God. You have distanced Yourself from us because of our iniquities. We have turned away from following after You, we have gone astray like sheep and have perished, and yet we have not returned from our wanderings.

Vehei'ach Na'iz Paneinu.	וְהֵיאַךְ נָעִיז פָּנֵינוּ.
Venaksheh Orpenu. Lomar	וְנַקְשֶׁה עָרְפֵּנוּ. לוֹמַר
Lefaneicha Adonai Eloheinu	לְפָנֶיךָ יְהֹוָה אֱלֹהֵינוּ
Velohei Avoteinu. Tzaddikim	וֵאלֹהֵי אֲבוֹתֵינוּ. צַדִּיקִים
Anachnu Velo Chatanu: (Aval	אֲנַחְנוּ וְלֹא חָטָאנוּ: (אֲבָל
Chatanu Anachnu Va'Avoteinu):	חָטָאנוּ אֲנַחְנוּ וַאֲבוֹתֵינוּ):

And how could we dare to lift our faces, stiffen our necks, and say before You, Hashem our God and God of our forefathers, we are righteous and have not sinned: (but in truth, we and our fathers have sinned)."

L'Adonai Eloheinu Harachamim	לַיְהֹוָה אֱלֹהֵינוּ הָרַחֲמִים
Vehasselichot, Ki Chatanu Lo:	וְהַסְּלִיחוֹת. כִּי חָטָאנוּ לוֹ:

To Hashem our God are mercy and forgiveness, for we have sinned against Him:

L'adonai Eloheinu Harachamim

לַיהוָה אֱלֹהֵינוּ הָרַחֲמִים

Vehasselichot, Ki Maradnu Bo:

וְהַסְּלִחוֹת. כִּי מָרַדְנוּ בּוֹ:

To Hashem our God are mercy and forgiveness, for we have rebelled against Him:

Al Na Tashet Aleinu Chatat,

אַל נָא תָשֵׁת עָלֵינוּ חַטָּאת.

Asher No'alnu Va'asher

אֲשֶׁר נוֹאַלְנוּ וַאֲשֶׁר

Chatanu:

חָטָאנוּ:

Please do not place upon us the sin that we have foolishly committed and which we sinned:

Chatanu Tzurenu. Selach Lanu

חָטָאנוּ צוּרֵנוּ. סְלַח לָנוּ

Yotzerenu:

יוֹצְרֵנוּ:

We have sinned, our Rock. Forgive us, our Creator.

Shema Yisra'el, Adonai

שְׁמַע יִשְׂרָאֵל. יְהוָה

Eloheinu, Adonai Echad:

אֱלֹהֵינוּ. יְהוָה אֶחָד:

Hear, Oh Yisrael, Hashem is our God, Hashem is One.

Adonai Hu ha'Elohim. Adonai

יְהוָה הוּא הָאֱלֹהִים. יְהוָה הוּא

Hu ha'Elohim: (Say Twice)

הָאֱלֹהִים: (ב' פעמים)

Hashem, He is God. Hashem, He is God. (Say twice)

Er'elei Ma'lah. Omerim Adonai
Adonenu. Bechirei Segullah.
Onim Ve'omerim. Adonai Hu
ha'Elohim. Adonai Hu
ha'Elohim:

אֶרְאֶלֵי מַעְלָה. אוֹמְרִים יְהֹוָה
אֲדוֹנֵנוּ. בְּחִירֵי סְגֻלָּה.
עוֹנִים וְאוֹמְרִים. יְהֹוָה הוּא
הָאֱלֹהִים. יְהֹוָה הוּא
הָאֱלֹהִים:

The angels on high say: Hashem is our Master. His chosen treasure,
respond and say: Hashem, He is God. Hashem, He is God.

Galgallei Ma'lah. Omerim
Adonai Adonenu. Degulei
Segullah. Onim Ve'omerim.
Adonai Hu ha'Elohim. Adonai
Hu ha'Elohim:

גַּלְגַּלֵּי מַעְלָה. אוֹמְרִים
יְהֹוָה אֲדוֹנֵנוּ. דְּגוּלֵי
סְגֻלָּה. עוֹנִים וְאוֹמְרִים.
יְהֹוָה הוּא הָאֱלֹהִים. יְהֹוָה
הוּא הָאֱלֹהִים:

The celestial spheres say: Hashem is our Master. The distinguished
treasures respond and say: Hashem, He is God. Hashem, He is God.

Hamonei Ma'lah. Omerim
Adonai Adonenu. Yisra'el
Betzaratam Uvegalutam Onim
Ve'omerim. Adonai Hu
ha'Elohim. Adonai Hu
ha'Elohim:

הֲמוֹנֵי מַעְלָה. אוֹמְרִים
יְהֹוָה אֲדוֹנֵנוּ. יִשְׂרָאֵל
בְּצָרָתָם וּבְגָלוּתָם עוֹנִים
וְאוֹמְרִים. יְהֹוָה הוּא
הָאֱלֹהִים. יְהֹוָה הוּא
הָאֱלֹהִים:

The multitudes on high say: Hashem is our Master. Yisrael, in their
distress and exile, respond and say: Hashem, He is God. Hashem,
He is God.

Adonai Melech. Adonai Malach.

Adonai Yimloch Le'olam Va'Ed:

יְהֹוָה מֶלֶךְ. יְהֹוָה מָלָךְ.
יְהֹוָה יִמְלֹךְ לְעוֹלָם וָעֶד:
(ב׳ פעמים)

(Say twice)

Hashem reigns. Hashem reigned. Hashem will reign forever and ever. (Say twice)

Beterem Shechakim Va'arakim

Nimtachu. Adonai Melech.

בְּטֶרֶם שְׁחָקִים וַאֲרָקִים
נִמְתָּחוּ. יְהֹוָה מֶלֶךְ.

Before the heavens and earth were stretched out, Hashem was King.

Ve'ad Lo Me'orot Zarachu.

Adonai Malach.

וְעַד לֹא מְאוֹרוֹת זָרָחוּ.
יְהֹוָה מָלָךְ.

And before the lights shone, Hashem reigned.

Veha'aretz Kabeged Tivleh.

Veshamayim Ke'ashan

Nimlachu. Adonai Yimloch

Le'olam Va'ed:

וְהָאָרֶץ כַּבֶּגֶד תִּבְלֶה.
וְשָׁמַיִם כְּעָשָׁן
נִמְלָחוּ. יְהֹוָה יִמְלֹךְ
לְעוֹלָם וָעֶד:

And when the earth will wear out like a garment, and the heavens will vanish like smoke, Hashem will reign forever and ever.

Some add:

Adonai Melech. Adonai Malach.

Adonai Yimloch Le'olam Va'ed:

יְהֹוָה מֶלֶךְ. יְהֹוָה מָלָךְ.
יְהֹוָה יִמְלֹךְ לְעוֹלָם וָעֶד:

Hashem reigns. Hashem reigned. Hashem will reign forever and ever.

Ve'ad Lo Asah Eretz Vechutzot.

Adonai Melech.

וְעַד לֹא עָשָׂה אֶרֶץ וְחוּצוֹת.

יְהֹוָה מֶלֶךְ.

And before He made the earth and its surroundings, Hashem was King.

Uvahachino Yetzurim Alei

Aratzot. Adonai Malach.

וּבַהֲכִינוֹ יְצוּרִים עֲלֵי

אֲרָצוֹת. יְהֹוָה מָלָךְ.

And when He prepared creation upon the lands, Hashem reigned.

Ve'et Yekabetz Nefutzim

Me'arba Tefutzot. Adonai

Yimloch Le'olam Va'ed:

וְעֵת יְקַבֵּץ נְפוּצִים

מֵאַרְבַּע תְּפוּצוֹת. יְהֹוָה

יִמְלֹךְ לְעוֹלָם וָעֶד:

And when He gathers the dispersed from the four corners, Hashem will reign forever and ever.

Some add:

Adonai Melech. Adonai Malach.

Adonai Yimloch Le'olam Va'ed:

יְהֹוָה מֶלֶךְ. יְהֹוָה מָלָךְ.

יְהֹוָה יִמְלֹךְ לְעוֹלָם וָעֶד:

Hashem reigns. Hashem reigned. Hashem will reign forever and ever.

Continue with Meyuchad on the next page.

Meyuchad

Meyuchad Be'ehyeh Asher	מְיוּחָד בְּאֶהְיֶה אֲשֶׁר
Ehyeh. Hu Hayah Vehu Hoveh	אֶהְיֶה. הוּא הָיָה וְהוּא הֹוֶה
Vehu Yihyeh. Hu Memit	וְהוּא יִהְיֶה. הוּא מֵמִית
Umechayeh. Lefanav Lo Notzar	וּמְחַיֶּה. לְפָנָיו לֹא נֹוצַר
El. Ve'acharav Lo Yihyeh:	אֵל. וְאַחֲרָיו לֹא יִהְיֶה:

Unique in "I will be what I will be." He was, He is, and He will be. He brings death and gives life. Before Him, no god was formed, and none will be after Him:

Echad Eloheinu. Gadol	אֶחָד אֱלֹהֵינוּ. גָּדֹול
Adonenu. Kadosh Venora	אֲדֹונֵנוּ. קָדֹושׁ וְנֹורָא
Shemo: Ki Gadol Me'al	שְׁמֹו: כִּי גָדֹול מֵעַל
Shamayim Chasdecha. Ve'ad	שָׁמַיִם חַסְדֶּךָ. וְעַד
Shechakim Amitecha: Ki Gadol	שְׁחָקִים אֲמִתֶּךָ: כִּי גָדֹול
Attah Ve'oseh Nifla'ot. Attah	אַתָּה וְעֹשֵׂה נִפְלָאֹות. אַתָּה
Elohim Levadecha: Shefoch	אֱלֹהִים לְבַדֶּךָ: שְׁפֹךְ
Chamatecha El Hagoyim Asher	חֲמָתְךָ אֶל הַגֹּויִם אֲשֶׁר
Lo Yeda'ucha. Ve'al Mamlachot.	לֹא יְדָעוּךָ. וְעַל מַמְלָכֹות.
Asher Beshimcha Lo Kara'u:	אֲשֶׁר בְּשִׁמְךָ לֹא קָרָאוּ:

Our God is One. Great is our Master. Holy and awesome is His Name. For Your loving-kindness is greater than the heavens, and Your truth reaches to the heavens. For You are great and do wonders; You alone are God. Pour out Your wrath upon the nations that do not know You, and upon the kingdoms that do not call on Your Name.

Likdushat Shimcha

Likdushat Shimcha Aseh Velo	לְקִדְשַׁת שִׁמְךָ עֲשֵׂה וְלֹא
Lanu: Lo Lanu Adonai Lo Lanu.	לָנוּ: לֹא לָנוּ יְהֹוָה לֹא לָנוּ.
Ki Leshimcha Ten Kavod. Al	כִּי לְשִׁמְךָ תֵּן כָּבוֹד. עַל
Chasdecha Al Amitecha: Lamah	חַסְדְּךָ עַל אֲמִתֶּךָ: לָמָּה
Yomru Hagoyim. Ayeh Na	יֹאמְרוּ הַגּוֹיִם. אַיֵּה נָא
Eloheihem: Veloheinu	אֱלֹהֵיהֶם: וֵאלֹהֵינוּ
Bashamayim. Echad Eloheinu	בַשָּׁמַיִם. אֶחָד אֱלֹהֵינוּ
Bashamayim. Edutenu Bechol	בַשָּׁמַיִם. עֵדוּתֵנוּ בְּכָל
Yom Pa'amayim. Chai Vekayam	יוֹם פַּעֲמַיִם. חַי וְקַיָם
Hu. Male Rachamim Hu. Male	הוּא. מְלֵא רַחֲמִים הוּא. מָלֵא
Zakiyut Hu. Kol Asher Chafetz	זַכִּיּוּת הוּא. כָּל אֲשֶׁר חָפֵץ
Asah Vashamayim Uva'aretz.	עָשָׂה בַשָּׁמַיִם וּבָאָרֶץ.
Ein Mi Yomar Lo Mah Ta'aseh.	אֵין מִי יֹאמַר לוֹ מַה תַּעֲשֶׂה.
Ve'ein Mi Yomar Lo Mah Tif'al.	וְאֵין מִי יֹאמַר לוֹ מַה תִּפְעָל.
Ki Hakol Ma'aseh Yadav:	כִּי הַכֹּל מַעֲשֵׂה יָדָיו:

For the sanctity of Your Name, act, and not for our sake. Not for our sake, Hashem, not for our sake, but for Your Name give glory, for Your loving-kindness and for Your truth. Why should the nations say, "Where is their God now?" And our God is in the heavens. Our God is One in the heavens. We testify twice every day. He is living and everlasting. He is full of mercy. He is full of merit. He has done all that He pleases in heaven and on earth. There is no one who can say to Him, "What are You doing?" And there is no one who can say to Him, "What will You do?" For everything is the work of His hands.

Continue with the series of Eloheinu Shebashamayim on the next page.

אֱלֹהֵינוּ שֶׁבַּשָּׁמַיִם שְׁמַע קוֹלֵנוּ וְקַבֵּל תְּפִלָּתֵנוּ בְּרָצוֹן:

Eloheinu Shebashamayim Shema Kolenu Vekabel Tefillatenu
Beratzon:

Our God in the heavens, hear our voice and accept our prayer with
favor:

אֱלֹהֵינוּ שֶׁבַּשָּׁמַיִם אַל תְּאַבְּדֵנוּ בְּאֹרֶךְ גָּלוּתֵנוּ:

Eloheinu Shebashamayim Al Te'abedenu Be'orech Galutenu:

Our God in the heavens, do not destroy us in our long exile:

(אֱלֹהֵינוּ שֶׁבַּשָּׁמַיִם) אַבֵּד כָּל הַקָּמִים עָלֵינוּ לְרָעָה:

Eloheinu Shebashamayim Abed Kol Hakamim Aleinu Lera'ah:

Our God in the heavens, destroy all who rise up against us for evil:

אֱלֹהֵינוּ שֶׁבַּשָּׁמַיִם בְּרִיתְךָ זְכֹר וְאַל תִּשְׁכָּחֵנוּ:

Eloheinu Shebashamayim Beritcha Zechor Ve'al Tishkachenu:

Our God in the heavens, remember Your covenant and do not
forget us:

אֱלֹהֵינוּ שֶׁבַּשָּׁמַיִם בָּרֵךְ אֶת לַחְמֵנוּ וְאֶת מֵימֵינוּ:

Eloheinu Shebashamayim Barech Et Lachmenu Ve'et Meimeinu:

Our God in the heavens, bless our bread and our water:

אֱלֹהֵינוּ שֶׁבַּשָּׁמַיִם בַּשְּׂרֵנוּ בְּשׂוֹרוֹת טוֹבוֹת:

Eloheinu Shebashamayim Basheorenu Besorot Tovot:

Our God in the heavens, announce good tidings to us:

אֱלֹהֵינוּ שֶׁבַּשָּׁמַיִם בַּטֵּל מֵעָלֵינוּ כָּל גְּזֵרוֹת קָשׁוֹת וְרָעוֹת:

Eloheinu Shebashamayim Battel Me'aleinu Kol Gezerot Kashot
Vera'ot:

Our God in the heavens, annul from upon us all harsh and evil
decrees:

אֱלֹהֵינוּ שֶׁבַּשָּׁמַיִם גְּזֹר עָלֵינוּ גְּזֵרוֹת טוֹבוֹת:

Eloheinu Shebashamayim Gezor Aleinu Gezerot Tovot:

Our God in the heavens, decree upon us good decrees:

אֱלֹהֵינוּ שֶׁבַּשָּׁמַיִם גַּלֵּה כְּבוֹד מַלְכוּתֶךָ עָלֵינוּ מְהֵרָה:

Eloheinu Shebashamayim Galleh Kevod Malchutecha Aleinu
Meherah:

Our God in the heavens, reveal the glory of Your kingdom upon us
quickly:

אֱלֹהֵינוּ שֶׁבַּשָּׁמַיִם דְּרַשְׁנוּךָ הִמָּצֵא לָנוּ:

Eloheinu Shebashamayim Derashnucha Himatze Lanu:

Our God in the heavens, when we seek You, find us:

אֱלֹהֵינוּ שֶׁבַּשָּׁמַיִם דְּרֹשׁ דָּמֵינוּ מִיַּד קָמֵינוּ:

Eloheinu Shebashamayim Derosh Dameinu Miyad Kameinu:

Our God in the heavens, seek our blood from the hands of our
enemies:

אֱלֹהֵינוּ שֶׁבַּשָּׁמַיִם הֵעָתֵר לָנוּ הַיּוֹם וּבְכָל יוֹם וָיוֹם בִּתְפִלָּתֵנוּ:

Eloheinu Shebashamayim He'ater Lanu Hayom Uvechol Yom Vayom
Bitfillatenu:

Our God in the heavens, incline to us today and every day in our
prayer:

אֱלֹהֵינוּ שֶׁבַּשָּׁמַיִם הַחֲזִירֵנוּ בִּתְשׁוּבָה שְׁלֵמָה לְפָנֶיךָ:

Eloheinu Shebashamayim Hachazirenu Bitshuvah Shelemah
Lefaneicha:

Our God in the heavens, return us in complete repentance before
You:

אֱלֹהֵינוּ שֶׁבַּשָּׁמַיִם וְאַל תְּבִישֵׁנוּ מִשִּׂבְרֵנוּ:

Eloheinu Shebashamayim Ve'al Tevishenu Mishioverenu:

Our God in the heavens, do not put us to shame because of our
brokenness:

אֱלֹהֵינוּ שֶׁבַּשָּׁמַיִם וְנִקְרָא וְאַתָּה תַעֲנֵנוּ:

Eloheinu Shebashamayim Venikra Ve'attah Ta'anenu:

Our God in the heavens, when we call answer us:

אֱלֹהֵינוּ שֶׁבַּשָּׁמַיִם זָכְרֵנוּ בְּזִכְרוֹן טוֹב מִלְּפָנֶיךָ:

Eloheinu Shebashamayim Zacherenu Bezichron Tov Millefaneicha:

Our God in the heavens, remember us with good remembrance
before You:

אֱלֹהֵינוּ שֶׁבַּשָּׁמַיִם זַכֵּנוּ בְּדִינֵנוּ:

Eloheinu Shebashamayim Zakenu Bedinenu:

Our God in the heavens, grant us merit in our judgment:

אֱלֹהֵינוּ שֶׁבַּשָּׁמַיִם חֲמֹל עָלֵינוּ וְעַל טַפֵּינוּ וְעַל עוֹלָלֵינוּ:

Eloheinu Shebashamayim Chamol Aleinu Ve'al Tapeinu Ve'al
Olaleinu:

Our God in the heavens, have compassion upon us and upon our
children and our infants:

אֱלֹהֵינוּ שֶׁבַּשָּׁמַיִם חוּס וְרַחֵם עָלֵינוּ:

Eloheinu Shebashamayim Chus Verachem Aleinu:

Our God in the heavens, have pity and mercy upon us:

אֱלֹהֵינוּ שֶׁבַּשָּׁמַיִם טַהֲרֵנוּ מֵעֲוֹנֵינוּ:

Eloheinu Shebashamayim Taharenu Me'avoneinu:

Our God in the heavens, purify us from our iniquities:

אֱלֹהֵינוּ שֶׁבַּשָּׁמַיִם טַהֲרֵנוּ מִטֻּמְאוֹתֵינוּ:

Eloheinu Shebashamayim Taharenu Mitum'oteinu:

Our God in the heavens, purify us from our impurities:

אֱלֹהֵינוּ שֶׁבַּשָּׁמַיִם יֶהֱמוּ נָא רַחֲמֶיךָ עָלֵינוּ:

Eloheinu Shebashamayim Yehemu Na Rachameicha Aleinu:

Our God in the heavens, let Your mercy be stirred upon us:

During the Ten Days of Repentance, add:

אֱלֹהֵינוּ שֶׁבַּשָּׁמַיִם כָּתְבֵנוּ בְּסֵפֶר חַיִּים טוֹבִים:

Eloheinu Shebashamayim Katevenu Besefer Chayim Tovim:

Our God in the heavens, inscribe us in the Book of Good Life:

אֱלֹהֵינוּ שֶׁבַּשָּׁמַיִם כָּתְבֵנוּ בְּסֵפֶר צַדִּיקִים וַחֲסִידִים:

Eloheinu Shebashamayim Katevenu Besefer Tzaddikim Vachasidim:

Our God in the heavens, inscribe us in the Book of the Righteous and Pious:

אֱלֹהֵינוּ שֶׁבַּשָּׁמַיִם כָּתְבֵנוּ בְּסֵפֶר יְשָׁרִים וּתְמִימִים:

Eloheinu Shebashamayim Katevenu Besefer Yesharim Utemimim:

Our God in the heavens, inscribe us in the Book of the Upright and Perfect:

אֱלֹהֵינוּ שֶׁבַּשָּׁמַיִם כָּתְבֵנוּ בְּסֵפֶר זָכִיּוֹת:

Eloheinu Shebashamayim Katevenu Besefer Zachiyot:

Our God in the heavens, inscribe us in the Book of Merits:

אֱלֹהֵינוּ שֶׁבַּשָּׁמַיִם כָּתְבֵנוּ בְּסֵפֶר מְזוֹנוֹת וּפַרְנָסָה טוֹבָה:

Eloheinu Shebashamayim Katevenu Besefer Mezonot Ufarnasah Tovah:

Our God in the heavens, inscribe us in the Book of Sustenance and Good Livelihood:

אֱלֹהֵינוּ שֶׁבַּשָּׁמַיִם כָּתְבֵנוּ בְּסֵפֶר מְחִילָה וּסְלִיחָה וְכַפָּרָה:

Eloheinu Shebashamayim Katevenu Besefer Mechilah Uselichah Vechapparah:

Our God in the heavens, inscribe us in the Book of Forgiveness, Pardon, and Atonement:

אֱלֹהֵינוּ שֶׁבַּשָּׁמַיִם כָּתְבֵנוּ בְּסֵפֶר גְּאֻלָּה וִישׁוּעָה:

Eloheinu Shebashamayim Katevenu Besefer Ge'ullah Vishu'ah:

Our God in the heavens, inscribe us in the Book of Redemption and Salvation:

אֱלֹהֵינוּ שֶׁבַּשָּׁמַיִם כְּבֹשׁ אֶת כּוֹבְשֵׁנוּ:

Eloheinu Shebashamayim Kevosh Et Koveshenu:

Our God in the heavens, subdue our oppressor:

אֱלֹהֵינוּ שֶׁבַּשָּׁמַיִם כָּלָה אַל תַּעַשׂ עִמָּנוּ:

Eloheinu Shebashamayim Kalah Al Ta'as Imanu:

Our God in the heavens, do not destroy us completely:

אֱלֹהֵינוּ שֶׁבַּשָּׁמַיִם לְמַעֲנָךְ עֲשֵׂה אִם לֹא לְמַעֲנֵנוּ:

Eloheinu Shebashamayim Lema'anach Aseh Im Lo Lema'anenu:

Our God in the heavens, act for Your sake if not for ours:

אֱלֹהֵינוּ שֶׁבַּשָּׁמַיִם לְחַץ אֶת לוֹחֲצֵינוּ:

Eloheinu Shebashamayim Lechatz Et Lochatzeinu:

Our God in the heavens, crush our oppressors:

אֱלֹהֵינוּ שֶׁבַּשָּׁמַיִם לְחַם אֶת לוֹחֲמֵינוּ:

Eloheinu Shebashamayim Lecham Et Lochameinu:

Our God in the heavens, fight our battles:

אֱלֹהֵינוּ שֶׁבַּשָּׁמַיִם מַלֵּא מִשְׁאֲלוֹת לִבֵּנוּ לְטוֹבָה לַעֲבוֹדָתֶךָ:

Eloheinu Shebashamayim Malle Mish'alot Libenu Letovah La'avodatecha:

Our God in the heavens, fulfill the desires of our heart for good in Your service:

אֱלֹהֵינוּ שֶׁבַּשָּׁמַיִם נְקֹם אֶת נִקְמָתֵנוּ:

Eloheinu Shebashamayim Nekom Et Nikmatenu:

Our God in the heavens, avenge our vengeance:

אֱלֹהֵינוּ שֶׁבַּשָּׁמַיִם סְמֹךְ אֶת נְפִילָתֵנוּ:

Eloheinu Shebashamayim Semoch Et Nefilatenu:

Our God in the heavens, support our fallen:

אֱלֹהֵינוּ שֶׁבַּשָּׁמַיִם סְמֹךְ אֶת סֻכַּת דָּוִד הַנּוֹפֶלֶת:

Eloheinu Shebashamayim Semoch Et Sukkat David Hanofelet:

Our God in the heavens, re-establish the fallen Sukkah of David:

אֱלֹהֵינוּ שֶׁבַּשָּׁמַיִם עֲנֵה אֶת עֲתִירָתֵנוּ:

Eloheinu Shebashamayim Aneh Et Atiratenu:

Our God in the heavens, answer our supplications:

אֱלֹהֵינוּ שֶׁבַּשָּׁמַיִם עֲנֵנוּ בְּיוֹם קָרְאֵנוּ:

Eloheinu Shebashamayim Anenu Beyom Kare'enu:

Our God in the heavens, answer us on the day we call:

אֱלֹהֵינוּ שֶׁבַּשָּׁמַיִם עֲנֵה אֶת מַעֲנֵנוּ:

Eloheinu Shebashamayim Aneh Et Me'anenu:

Our God in the heavens, answer our petitions:

אֱלֹהֵינוּ שֶׁבַּשָּׁמַיִם פְּדֵנוּ מִידֵי כָל אוֹיְבֵינוּ:

Eloheinu Shebashamayim Pedenu Midei Chol Oyeveinu:

Our God in heaven, redeem us from the hands of all our enemies:

אֱלֹהֵינוּ שֶׁבַּשָּׁמַיִם פְּדֵנוּ מִידֵי יִצְרֵנוּ הָרַע:

Eloheinu Shebashamayim Pedenu Midei Yitzrenu Hara:

Our God in the heavens, redeem us from the hands of our evil inclination:

אֱלֹהֵינוּ שֶׁבַּשָּׁמַיִם צַוֵּה אִתָּנוּ בִּרְכוֹתֶיךָ:

Eloheinu Shebashamayim Tzaveh Itanu Birchoteicha:

Our God in the heavens, command for us Your blessings:

אֱלֹהֵינוּ שֶׁבַּשָּׁמַיִם צַוֵּה אִתָּנוּ יְשׁוּעוֹתֶיךָ:

Eloheinu Shebashamayim Tzaveh Itanu Yeshu'oteicha:

Our God in the heavens, command for us Your salvations:

אֱלֹהֵינוּ שֶׁבַּשָּׁמַיִם צַדְּקֵנוּ בְּמִשְׁפָּטֶיךָ:

Eloheinu Shebashamayim Tzaddekenu Bemishpateicha:

Our God in the heavens, justify us with Your judgment:

אֱלֹהֵינוּ שֶׁבַּשָּׁמַיִם קָרֵב לָנוּ קֵץ הַגְּאֻלָּה:

Eloheinu Shebashamayim Karev Lanu Ketz Hage'ullah:

Our God in heaven, bring us closer to the end of the redemption:

אֱלֹהֵינוּ שֶׁבַּשָּׁמַיִם קָרֵב לָנוּ יוֹם הַיְשׁוּעָה:

Eloheinu Shebashamayim Karev Lanu Yom Hayeshu'ah:

Our God in the heavens, bring us closer to the day of salvation:

אֱלֹהֵינוּ שֶׁבַּשָּׁמַיִם קָרְבֵנוּ לַעֲבוֹדָתֶךָ:

Eloheinu Shebashamayim Karevenu La'avodatecha:

Our God in the heavens, bring us near to Your service:

אֱלֹהֵינוּ שֶׁבַּשָּׁמַיִם רִיבָה רִיבֵנוּ וּגְאָלֵנוּ:

Eloheinu Shebashamayim Rivah Rivenu Uge'alenu:

Our God in the heavens, fight our fight and redeem us:

אֱלֹהֵינוּ שֶׁבַּשָּׁמַיִם רְאֵה בָעֳנִי עַמְּךָ יִשְׂרָאֵל:

Eloheinu Shebashamayim Re'eh Bo'oni Ammecha Yisra'el:

Our God in the heavens, see the suffering of Your people Yisrael:

אֱלֹהֵינוּ שֶׁבַּשָּׁמַיִם רְפָא כָּל חוֹלֵי עַמְּךָ יִשְׂרָאֵל:

Eloheinu Shebashamayim Refa Kol Cholei Ammecha Yisra'el:
Our God in the heavens, heal all the sick of Your people Yisrael:

אֱלֹהֵינוּ שֶׁבַּשָּׁמַיִם רְאֵה בְּדֹחַק הַשָּׁעָה:

Eloheinu Shebashamayim Re'eh Bedochak Hasha'ah:
Our God in the heavens, see the urgency of the hour:

אֱלֹהֵינוּ שֶׁבַּשָּׁמַיִם שְׁעֵה אֶת שַׁוְעָתֵנוּ:

Eloheinu Shebashamayim She'eh Et Shav'atenu:
Our God in the heavens, hear our cry:

אֱלֹהֵינוּ שֶׁבַּשָּׁמַיִם שִׁית שָׁלוֹם בֵּינֵינוּ:

Eloheinu Shebashamayim Shit Shalom Beineinu:
Our God in the heavens, establish peace between us:

אֱלֹהֵינוּ שֶׁבַּשָׁמַיִם שִׁית שַׁלְוָה בְּאַרְמְנוֹתֵינוּ:

Eloheinu Shebashamayim Shit Shalvah Be'armenoteinu:
Our God in the heavens, establish tranquility in our dwellings:

אֱלֹהֵינוּ שֶׁבַּשָּׁמַיִם תֵּן שָׁלוֹם בָּאָרֶץ:

Eloheinu Shebashamayim Ten Shalom Ba'aretz:
Our God in the heavens grant peace in the land:

אֱלֹהֵינוּ שֶׁבַּשָּׁמַיִם תֵּן שָׂבָע בָּעוֹלָם:

Eloheinu Shebashamayim Ten Sava Ba'olam:
Our God in the heavens, grant abundance in the world:

אֱלֹהֵינוּ שֶׁבַּשָּׁמַיִם תֵּן שָׁלוֹם בַּמַּלְכוּת:

Eloheinu Shebashamayim Ten Shalom Bamalchut:
Our God in the heavens, grant peace to the government:

אֱלֹהֵינוּ שֶׁבַּשָּׁמַיִם תֵּן טַל וּמָטָר לִבְרָכָה בְּעִתּוֹ בָּאָרֶץ:

Eloheinu Shebashamayim Ten Tal Umatar Livrachah Be'ito Ba'aretz:

Our God in the heavens, grant dew and rain for blessing in their season on the land:

אֱלֹהֵינוּ שֶׁבַּשָּׁמַיִם תֵּן זֶרַע לַזּוֹרֵעַ וְלֶחֶם לָאוֹכֵל:

Eloheinu Shebashamayim Ten Zera Lazorea' Velechem La'ochel:

Our God in the heavens, grant seed for the sower and bread for the eater:

אֱלֹהֵינוּ שֶׁבַּשָּׁמַיִם תֵּן לֶחֶם לְפִי הַטַּף לָשֹׂבַע:

Eloheinu Shebashamayim Ten Lechem Lefi Hataf Lasva:

Our God in the heavens, provide bread for the mouths of the young for satisfaction:

אֱלֹהֵינוּ שֶׁבַּשָּׁמַיִם תִּכּוֹן תְּפִלָּתֵנוּ קְטֹרֶת לְפָנֶיךָ:

Eloheinu Shebashamayim Tikon Tefillatenu Ketoret Lefaneicha:

Our God in the heavens, establish our prayer as an incense-offering before You:

Eloheinu Shebashamayim Aseh	אֱלֹהֵינוּ שֶׁבַּשָּׁמַיִם עֲשֵׂה
Imanu Ot Letovah. Aseh Imanu	עִמָּנוּ אוֹת לְטוֹבָה. עֲשֵׂה עִמָּנוּ
Ot Lishu'ah. Aseh Imanu Ot	אוֹת לִישׁוּעָה. עֲשֵׂה עִמָּנוּ אוֹת
Lerachamim. Yir'u Sone'einu	לְרַחֲמִים. יִרְאוּ שׂוֹנְאֵינוּ
Veyevoshu. Yechezu Oyeveinu	וְיֵבֹשׁוּ. יֶחֱזוּ אוֹיְבֵינוּ
Veyikalemu. Ki Attah Adonai	וְיִכָּלְמוּ. כִּי אַתָּה יְהֹוָה
Azartanu Venichamtanu:	עֲזַרְתָּנוּ וְנִחַמְתָּנוּ:

Our God in heaven, make a sign of goodness for us. Make a sign of salvation for us. Make a sign of mercy for us. Let our enemies see and be ashamed. Let our adversaries see and be confounded. For You, Hashem, have helped us and comforted us.

Berogez Rachem Tizkor.	בְּרֹגֶז רַחֵם תִּזְכֹּר.
Berogez Ahavah Tizkor. Berogez	בְּרֹגֶז אַהֲבָה תִּזְכֹּר. בְּרֹגֶז
Akedah Tizkor. Berogez	עֲקֵדָה תִּזְכֹּר. בְּרֹגֶז
Temimut Tizkor. Habet Laberit	תְּמִימוּת תִּזְכֹּר. הַבֵּט לַבְּרִית
Ve'al Tafer Beritcha Itanu.	וְאַל תָּפֵר בְּרִיתְךָ אִתָּנוּ.
Anenu Va'et Uva'onah Hazot:	עֲנֵנוּ בָעֵת וּבָעוֹנָה הַזֹּאת:

In wrath, recall mercy. In wrath, recall love. In wrath, recall the binding. In wrath, recall innocence. Look to the covenant and do not annul your covenant with us. Answer us at this time and in this season:

Some say:

אֱלֹהִים אַתָּה יָדַעְתָּ לְאִוַּלְתִּי וְאַשְׁמוֹתַי. מִמְּךָ לֹא נִכְחֲדוּ כָּל זְדוֹנוֹתַי.
בְּהַעֲלוֹתִי עַל לְבָבִי גֹּדֶל מְשׁוּבוֹתַי. (כְּמַיִם נִשְׁפַּכְתִּי וְהִתְפָּרְדוּ כָּל
עַצְמוֹתַי.) הַקְשִׁיבָה בְּקוֹל תַּחֲנוּנוֹתַי: רַחֵם בְּרֹגֶז תִּזְכֹּר לְדוֹפֵק שַׁעֲרֵי
חֶמְלָתֶךָ. הָעוֹמֵד כְּדַל שׁוֹאֵל מְבַקֵּשׁ סְלִיחָתֶךָ. קִדְּמוּ עֵינַי אַשְׁמוּרוֹת
לְסַפֵּר גְּדֻלָּתֶךָ. אַגִּיד זְרוֹעֶךָ לְדוֹר לְכָל יָבוֹא גְּבוּרָתֶךָ: גַּל עֵינַי
וְאַבִּיטָה מִתּוֹרָתְךָ נִפְלָאוֹת. יְזַמְּרוּ לְשִׁמְךָ מְיַחֲלֵי קֵץ
פְּלָאוֹת. תְּשׁוֹבֵב לִנְוֵיהֶם פְּזוּרִים בְּכָל פֵּאוֹת. כִּי אַתָּה יהוה אֱלֹהִים
צְבָאוֹת: אֱלֹהִים צְבָאוֹת הֲשִׁיבֵנוּ. נוֹרָאוֹת בְּצֶדֶק תַּעֲנֵנוּ. הַבֵּט פְּנֵי
מְשִׁיחֶךָ וּרְאֵה מָגִנֵּנוּ. וְיִשְׂמְחוּ כָל חוֹסֵי בָךְ לְעוֹלָם יְרַנֵּנוּ. עֲנֵנוּ
אָבִינוּ עֲנֵנוּ:

Elohim Attah Yada'ta Le'ivalti Ve'ashmotai. Mimecha Lo Nichchadu
Kol Zedonotai. Beha'aloti Al Levavi Godel Meshuvotai. (Kamayim
Nishpachti Vehitparedu Kol Atzmotai.) Hakshivah Vekol
Tachanunotai: Rachem Berogez Tizkor Ledofek Sha'arei
Chemlatecha. Ha'omed Kedal Sho'el Mevakesh Selichatecha.
Kiddemu Einai Ashmurot Lesaper Gedullatecha. Aggid Zero'acha
Ledor Lechol Yavo Gevuratecha: Gal Einai Ve'abitah Mitoratecha
Nifla'ot. Yezammeru Leshimcha Meyachalei Ketz Pela'ot. Teshovev
Linveihem Pezurim Bechol Pe'ot. Ki Attah Adonai Elohim

Tzeva'ot: Elohim Tzeva'ot Hashivenu. Nora'ot Betzedek Ta'anenu. Habet Penei Meshichecha Ure'eh Maginenu. Veyismechu Chol Chosei Vach Le'olam Yeranenu. Anenu Avinu Anenu:

God, You knew of my foolishness, and my guilt was not hidden from you. All my transgressions are revealed. When I contemplate in my heart, my sins are numerous. (Like water, I am poured out, and all my bones were scattered.) Listen to the sound of my supplications: In anger, remember Your gates of mercy. He who stands like a beggar asks for Your forgiveness. My eyes anticipate the night watches to tell of Your greatness. I will proclaim Your might to a generation, Your strength to all generations that will come. Uncover my eyes, and I will behold the wonders of Your Torah. Those who wait for the end shall praise your name for the wonders. Restore the scattered ones to their homes, in all corners of the earth. For you are Hashem, God of hosts. God of hosts, restore us. Answer us with awesome deeds of righteousness. Look upon the face of Your anointed and see to our protection. And let all who trust in You rejoice, they will sing forever. Answer us, our Father, answer us.

Aneinu

Anenu Avinu Anenu. Anenu	עֲנֵנוּ אָבִינוּ עֲנֵנוּ. עֲנֵנוּ
Bore'enu Anenu. Anenu	בּוֹרְאֵנוּ עֲנֵנוּ. עֲנֵנוּ
Go'alenu Anenu. Anenu	גּוֹאֲלֵנוּ עֲנֵנוּ. עֲנֵנוּ
Doreshenu Anenu. Anenu Hod	דּוֹרְשֵׁנוּ עֲנֵנוּ. עֲנֵנוּ הוֹד
Vehadar Anenu. Anenu Vatik	וְהָדָר עֲנֵנוּ. עֲנֵנוּ וָתִיק
Benechamot Anenu. Anenu Zach	בְּנֶחָמוֹת עֲנֵנוּ. עֲנֵנוּ זַךְ
Veyashar Anenu. Anenu Chai	וְיָשָׁר עֲנֵנוּ. עֲנֵנוּ חַי
Vekayam Anenu. Anenu Tehor	וְקַיָם עֲנֵנוּ. עֲנֵנוּ טָהוֹר
Einayim Anenu. Anenu Yoshev	עֵינַיִם עֲנֵנוּ. עֲנֵנוּ יוֹשֵׁב
Shamayim Anenu. Anenu Kabir	שָׁמַיִם עֲנֵנוּ. עֲנֵנוּ כַּבִּיר

Koach Anenu. Anenu Lo El	כֹּחַ עֲנֵנוּ. עֲנֵנוּ לֹא אֵל
Chafetz Beresha Anenu. Anenu	חָפֵץ בְּרֶשַׁע עֲנֵנוּ. עֲנֵנוּ
Melech Malchei Hamelachim	מֶלֶךְ מַלְכֵי הַמְּלָכִים
Anenu. Anenu Nora Venisgav	עֲנֵנוּ. עֲנֵנוּ נוֹרָא וְנִשְׂגָּב
Anenu. Anenu Somech Nofelim	עֲנֵנוּ. עֲנֵנוּ סוֹמֵךְ נוֹפְלִים
Anenu. Anenu Ozer Dallim	עֲנֵנוּ. עֲנֵנוּ עוֹזֵר דַּלִּים
Anenu. Anenu Podeh Umatzil	עֲנֵנוּ. עֲנֵנוּ פּוֹדֶה וּמַצִּיל
Anenu. Anenu Tzaddik	עֲנֵנוּ. עֲנֵנוּ צַדִּיק
Umatzdik Anenu. Anenu Karov	וּמַצְדִּיק עֲנֵנוּ. עֲנֵנוּ קָרוֹב
Lechol Kore'av Be'emet Anenu.	לְכָל קוֹרְאָיו בֶּאֱמֶת עֲנֵנוּ.
Anenu Ram Venisa Anenu.	עֲנֵנוּ רָם וְנִשָּׂא עֲנֵנוּ.
Anenu Shochen Shechakim	עֲנֵנוּ שׁוֹכֵן שְׁחָקִים
Anenu. Anenu Tomech Temimim	עֲנֵנוּ. עֲנֵנוּ תּוֹמֵךְ תְּמִימִים
Anenu:	עֲנֵנוּ:

Answer us, our Father, answer us. Answer us, our Creator, answer us. Answer us, our Redeemer, answer us. Answer us, our Seeker, answer us. Answer us, Glory and Splendor, answer us. Answer us, the Eternal Comforter, answer us. Answer us, pure and upright, answer us. Answer us, living and enduring, answer us. Answer us, the One with pure eyes, answer us. Answer us, He Who dwells in heaven, answer us. Answer us, the great in strength, answer us. Answer us, the God Who does not desire wickedness, answer us. Answer us, the King of kings, answer us. Answer us, awesome and exalted, answer us. Answer us, the Supporter of the fallen, answer us. Answer us, the Helper of the poor, answer us. Answer us, the Redeemer and Deliverer, answer us. Answer us, the Righteous and Justifier, answer us. Answer us, close to all who call upon Him in truth, answer us. Answer us, the Exalted and Uplifted, answer us. Answer us, the Dweller of the heavens, answer us. Answer us, the Supporter of the innocent, answer us.

Anenu Elohei Avraham Anenu: עֲנֵנוּ אֱלֹהֵי אַבְרָהָם עֲנֵנוּ:

Anenu Ufachad Yitzchak Anenu: עֲנֵנוּ וּפַחַד יִצְחָק עֲנֵנוּ:

Anenu Avir Ya'akov Anenu: עֲנֵנוּ אֲבִיר יַעֲקֹב עֲנֵנוּ:

Anenu Magen David Anenu: עֲנֵנוּ מָגֵן דָּוִד עֲנֵנוּ:

Anenu Ha'oneh Be'et Ratzon עֲנֵנוּ הָעוֹנֶה בְּעֵת רָצוֹן

Anenu: Anenu Ha'oneh Be'et עֲנֵנוּ: עֲנֵנוּ הָעוֹנֶה בְּעֵת

Tzarah Anenu: Anenu Ha'oneh צָרָה עֲנֵנוּ: עֲנֵנוּ הָעוֹנֶה

Be'et Rachamim Anenu: Anenu בְּעֵת רַחֲמִים עֲנֵנוּ: עֲנֵנוּ

Elohei Hamerkavah Anenu: אֱלֹהֵי הַמֶּרְכָּבָה עֲנֵנוּ:

Some Add: Anenu Elaha Deme'ir Anenu: יש המוסיפים: עֲנֵנוּ אֱלָהָא דְמֵאִיר עֲנֵנוּ:

Anenu Bizchuteh Devar-Yocha Anenu: עֲנֵנוּ בִּזְכוּתֵהּ דְּבַר־יוֹחַאי עֲנֵנוּ:

Anenu Mishogav Ha'imahot Anenu: עֲנֵנוּ מִשְׂגָּב הָאִמָּהוֹת עֲנֵנוּ:

Anenu Ezrat Hashevatim Anenu: עֲנֵנוּ עֶזְרַת הַשְּׁבָטִים עֲנֵנוּ:

Anenu Rachum Vechanun עֲנֵנוּ רַחוּם וְחַנּוּן

Anenu: עֲנֵנוּ:

Answer us, God of Avraham, answer us; answer us and the fear of Yitzchak, answer us; answer us, Mighty One of Yaakov, answer us; answer us, Shield of David, answer us; answer us, the One Who responds at the time of favor, answer us; answer us, the One Who responds during times of trouble, answer us; answer us, the One Who responds at the time of mercy, answer us; answer us, God of the chariot, **some add:** answer us; answer us, the God of Meir, answer us; answer us in the merit of Bar-Yochai, answer us; answer us from the refuge of the matriarchs, answer us; answer us, the helper of the tribes, answer us; Answer us, compassionate and gracious, answer us.

Rachum Vechanun Chatanu Lefaneicha רַחוּם וְחַנּוּן חָטָאנוּ

Rachem Aleinu: לְפָנֶיךָ רַחֵם עָלֵינוּ:

Compassionate and gracious, we have sinned before You; have mercy upon us.

Adon Haselichot

Adon Hasselichot. Bochen	אֲדוֹן הַסְּלִיחוֹת. בּוֹחֵן
Levavot. Goleh Amukot. Dover	לְבָבוֹת. גּוֹלֶה עֲמוּקוֹת. דּוֹבֵר
Tzedakot. Chatanu Lefaneicha	צְדָקוֹת. חָטָאנוּ לְפָנֶיךָ
Rachem Aleinu: Hadur	רַחֵם עָלֵינוּ: הָדוּר
Benifla'ot. Vatik Benechamot.	בְּנִפְלָאוֹת. וָתִיק בְּנֶחָמוֹת.
Zocher Berit Avot. Choker	זוֹכֵר בְּרִית אָבוֹת. חוֹקֵר
Kelayot: Chatanu Lefaneicha	כְּלָיוֹת: חָטָאנוּ לְפָנֶיךָ
Rachem Aleinu: Tov Umetiv	רַחֵם עָלֵינוּ: טוֹב וּמֵטִיב
Laberiyot. Yodea' Kol Nistarot.	לַבְּרִיּוֹת. יוֹדֵעַ כָּל נִסְתָּרוֹת.
Kovesh Avonot. Lovesh	כּוֹבֵשׁ עֲוֹנוֹת. לוֹבֵשׁ
Tzedakot: Chatanu Lefaneicha	צְדָקוֹת: חָטָאנוּ לְפָנֶיךָ
Rachem Aleinu: Male Zakiyut.	רַחֵם עָלֵינוּ: מָלֵא זַכִּיּוּת.
Nora Tehillot. Soleach Avonot.	נוֹרָא תְהִלּוֹת. סוֹלֵחַ עֲוֹנוֹת.
Oneh Be'et Tzarot: Chatanu	עוֹנֶה בְּעֵת צָרוֹת: חָטָאנוּ
Lefaneicha Rachem Aleinu:	לְפָנֶיךָ רַחֵם עָלֵינוּ:
Po'el Yeshu'ot. Tzofeh Atidot.	פּוֹעֵל יְשׁוּעוֹת. צוֹפֶה עֲתִידוֹת.
Kore Hadorot. Rochev Aravot.	קוֹרֵא הַדּוֹרוֹת. רוֹכֵב עֲרָבוֹת.
Shomea' Tefillot. Temim De'ot:	שׁוֹמֵעַ תְּפִלּוֹת. תְּמִים דֵּעוֹת:
Chatanu Lefaneicha Rachem	חָטָאנוּ לְפָנֶיךָ רַחֵם
Aleinu: El Rachum Shimcha. El	עָלֵינוּ: אֵל רַחוּם שְׁמֶךָ. אֵל
Chanun Shimcha. El Erech	חַנּוּן שְׁמֶךָ. אֵל אֶרֶךְ
Apayim Shimcha. Male	אַפַּיִם שְׁמֶךָ. מָלֵא
Rachamim Shimcha. Banu	רַחֲמִים שְׁמֶךָ. בָּנוּ
Nikra Shimcha. Adonai Aseh	נִקְרָא שְׁמֶךָ. יְהֹוָה עֲשֵׂה
Lema'an Shemecha:	לְמַעַן שְׁמֶךָ:

Master of forgiveness, Examiner of hearts, Revealer of hidden secrets, Speaker of righteousness, **we have sinned before You, have mercy upon us**; Majestic in wonders, Eternal in consolations, Who remembers the covenant with our forefathers, examiner of kidneys (motives): **we have sinned before You, have mercy upon us**; good and Benefactor of creations, Knower of all hidden things, Subduer of sins, Adorned in righteousness: **we have sinned before You, have mercy upon us**; Full of merits, Awesome in praises, Forgiver of sins, Responder during times of distress: **we have sinned before You, have mercy upon us**; Performer of salvations, Seer of futures, Caller of generations, Rider of clouds, Listener of prayers, Perfect in knowledge: **we have sinned before You, have mercy upon us**; Merciful God is Your name, Gracious God is Your name, Slow to anger is Your name, Full of mercy is Your name, Your name is called on us, Hashem, act for the sake of Your name.

During the Ten Days of Repentance, some add:

El Rachum Shemach. El Chanun
Shemach. Re'eh Bo'oni
Ammach. Rachem Al Olamach:

אֵל רַחוּם שְׁמָךְ. אֵל חַנּוּן
שְׁמָךְ. רְאֵה בְעָנְיִ
עַמָּךְ. רַחֵם עַל עוֹלָמָךְ:

Your name is Merciful God. Your name is Gracious God. Look upon the suffering of Your people. Have mercy on Your world.

El Addir Shemach. El Baruch
Shemach. El Gadol Shemach. El
Dagul Shemach: Re'eh Bo'oni
Ammach. Rachem Al Olamach:

אֵל אַדִּיר שְׁמָךְ. אֵל בָּרוּךְ
שְׁמָךְ. אֵל גָּדוֹל שְׁמָךְ. אֵל
דָּגוּל שְׁמָךְ: רְאֵה בְעָנְיִ
עַמָּךְ. רַחֵם עַל עוֹלָמָךְ:

Your name is Mighty God. Your name is Blessed God. Your name is Great God. Your name is Distinguished God. Look upon the suffering of Your people. Have mercy on Your world.

El Hadur Shemach. El Vatik	אֵל הָדוּר שְׁמָךְ. אֵל וָתִיק
Shemach. El Zaka Shemach. El	שְׁמָךְ. אֵל זַכַּאי שְׁמָךְ. אֵל חוֹנֵן
Chonen Shemach: Re'eh Bo'oni	שְׁמָךְ: רְאֵה בָעֳנִי עַמָּךְ. רַחֵם
Ammach. Rachem Al Olamach:	עַל עוֹלָמָךְ:

Your name is Majestic God. Your name is Eternal God. Your name is Meritorious God. Your name is Gracious God. Look upon the suffering of Your people. Have mercy on Your world:

El Tahor Shemach. El Yachid	אֵל טָהוֹר שְׁמָךְ. אֵל יָחִיד
Shemach. El Kabir Shemach. El	שְׁמָךְ. אֵל כַּבִּיר שְׁמָךְ. אֵל
La'ad Shemach: Re'eh Bo'oni	לָעַד שְׁמָךְ: רְאֵה בָעֳנִי
Ammach. Rachem Al Olamach:	עַמָּךְ. רַחֵם עַל עוֹלָמָךְ:

Your name is Pure God. Your name is Unique God. Your name is Mighty God. Your name is Eternal God. Look upon the suffering of Your people. Have mercy on Your world:

El Melech Shemach. El Nora	אֵל מֶלֶךְ שְׁמָךְ. אֵל נוֹרָא
Shemach. El Somech Shemach.	שְׁמָךְ. אֵל סוֹמֵךְ שְׁמָךְ.
El Ozer Shemach: Re'eh Bo'oni	אֵל עוֹזֵר שְׁמָךְ: רְאֵה בָעֳנִי
Ammach. Rachem Al Olamach:	עַמָּךְ. רַחֵם עַל עוֹלָמָךְ:

Your name is King God. Your name is Awesome God. Your name is Supporting God. Your name is Helper God. Look upon the suffering of Your people. Have mercy on Your world:

El Podeh Shemach. El Tzaddik	אֵל פּוֹדֶה שְׁמָךְ. אֵל צַדִּיק
Shemach. El Kadosh Shemach.	שְׁמָךְ. אֵל קָדוֹשׁ שְׁמָךְ.
El Rachman Shemach: Re'eh	אֵל רַחְמָן שְׁמָךְ: רְאֵה
Bo'oni Ammach. Rachem Al	בָעֳנִי עַמָּךְ. רַחֵם עַל
Olamach:	עוֹלָמָךְ:

Your name is Redeemer God. Your name is Righteous God. Your name is Holy God. Your name is Merciful God. Look upon the suffering of Your people. Have mercy on Your world:

El Shaddai Shemach. El Shomer	אֵל שַׁדַּי שְׁמָךְ. אֵל שׁוֹמֵר
Shemach. El Tomech Shemach.	שְׁמָךְ. אֵל תּוֹמֵךְ שְׁמָךְ.
El Tamim Shemach: Re'eh	אֵל תָּמִים שְׁמָךְ: רְאֵה
Bo'oni Ammach. Rachem Al	בָּעֳנִי עַמָּךְ. רַחֵם עַל
Olamach:	עוֹלָמָךְ:

Your name is El Shaddai. Your name is Guardian God. Your name is Sustaining God. Your name is Perfect God. Look upon the suffering of Your people. Have mercy on Your world:

During the Ten Days of Repentance, say:

Adonai Chonenu Vahakimenu,	יְהֹוָה חָנֵּנוּ וַהֲקִימֵנוּ.
Uvesefer Chayim Zacherenu	וּבְסֵפֶר חַיִּים זָכְרֵנוּ
Vechatevenu:	וְכָתְבֵנוּ:

Hashem, be gracious to us and raise us up, and remember us and inscribe us in the Book of Life.

Adonai Beyom Yeshu'atah	יְהֹוָה בְּיוֹם יְשׁוּעָתָה
Basrenu Verachamenu, Uvesefer	בַּשְּׂרֵנוּ וְרַחֲמֵנוּ. וּבְסֵפֶר
Chayim Zacherenu	חַיִּים זָכְרֵנוּ
Vechatevenu:	וְכָתְבֵנוּ:

Hashem, on the day of salvation, announce to us and have mercy on us, and remember us and inscribe us in the Book of Life.

Adonai Galgel Hamon   יְהֹוָה גַּלְגֵּל הָמוֹן

Rachameicha Aleinu, Uvesefer   רַחֲמֶיךָ עָלֵינוּ. וּבְסֵפֶר

Chayim Zacherenu   חַיִּים זָכְרֵנוּ

Vechatevenu: וְכָתְבֵנוּ:

Hashem, arouse the abundance of Your mercies upon us, and remember us and inscribe us in the Book of Life.

Adonai Yehemu Na   יְהֹוָה יֶהֱמוּ נָא

Rachameicha Aleinu, Uvesefer   רַחֲמֶיךָ עָלֵינוּ. וּבְסֵפֶר

Chayim Zacherenu   חַיִּים זָכְרֵנוּ

Vechatevenu: וְכָתְבֵנוּ:

Hashem, let Your mercies be stirred upon us, and remember us and inscribe us in the Book of Life.

Adonai Kachotam Al Lev   יְהֹוָה כְּחוֹתָם עַל לֵב

Hayom Simenu, Uvesefer   הַיּוֹם שִׂימֵנוּ. וּבְסֵפֶר

Chayim Zacherenu   חַיִּים זָכְרֵנוּ

Vechatevenu: וְכָתְבֵנוּ:

Hashem, set us as a seal on Your heart today, and remember us and inscribe us in the Book of Life.

Adonai Rivah Rivenu Ulecham   יְהֹוָה רִיבָה רִיבֵנוּ וּלְחַם

Lochameinu, Uvesefer Chayim   לוֹחֲמֵינוּ. וּבְסֵפֶר חַיִּים

Zacherenu Vechatevenu: זָכְרֵנוּ וְכָתְבֵנוּ:

Hashem, contend our cause and fight our battles, and remember us and inscribe us in the Book of Life.

Adonai Barech Et Lachmenu

Ve'et Meimeinu, Uvesefer

Chayim Zacherenu

Vechatevenu:

יְהֹוָה בָּרֵךְ אֶת לַחְמֵנוּ וְאֶת
מֵימֵינוּ. וּבְסֵפֶר חַיִּים זָכְרֵנוּ
וְכָתְבֵנוּ:

Hashem, bless our bread and our water, and remember us and
inscribe us in the Book of Life.

Adonai Aseh Lema'an

Shemecha, Vechusah Al Yisra'el

Ammecha:

יְהֹוָה עֲשֵׂה לְמַעַן
שְׁמֶךָ. וְחוּסָה עַל יִשְׂרָאֵל
עַמֶּךָ:

Hashem, act for the sake of Your name, and have compassion on
Yisrael, Your people:

Adonai Aseh Lema'an Avraham

Ezrach Temimecha, Vechusah Al

Yisra'el Ammecha:

יְהֹוָה עֲשֵׂה לְמַעַן אַבְרָהָם
אֶזְרַח תְּמִימֶךָ. וְחוּסָה עַל
יִשְׂרָאֵל עַמֶּךָ:

Hashem, act for the sake of Avraham, Your perfect servant, and
have compassion on Yisrael, Your people:

Adonai Aseh Lema'an Yitzchak

Ne'ekad Be'ulamecha,

Vechusah Al Yisra'el Ammecha:

יְהֹוָה עֲשֵׂה לְמַעַן יִצְחָק
נֶעֱקַד בְּאוּלַמֶּךָ.
וְחוּסָה עַל יִשְׂרָאֵל עַמֶּךָ:

Hashem, act for the sake of Yitzchak, who was bound on Your altar,
and have compassion on Yisrael, Your people:

Adonai Aseh Lema'an Ya'akov

Ne'enah Vesullam

Mimeromeicha, Vechusah Al

Yisra'el Ammecha:

יְהֹוָה עֲשֵׂה לְמַעַן יַעֲקֹב

נֶעֱנָה בְסֻלָּם

מִמְּרוֹמֶיךָ. וְחוּסָה עַל

יִשְׂרָאֵל עַמֶּךָ:

Hashem, act for the sake of Yaakov, who was answered with the ladder from Your heights, and have compassion on Yisrael, Your people:

Adonai Aseh Lema'an Mosheh

Ne'eman Bechol Beitecha,

Vechusah Al Yisra'el Ammecha:

יְהֹוָה עֲשֵׂה לְמַעַן מֹשֶׁה

נֶאֱמָן בְּכָל בֵּיתֶךָ.

וְחוּסָה עַל יִשְׂרָאֵל עַמֶּךָ:

Hashem, act for the sake of Moshe, who was faithful in all of Your house, and have compassion on Yisrael, Your people:

Adonai Aseh Lema'an Aharon

Kihen Be'ureicha Vetumeicha,

Vechusah Al Yisra'el Ammecha:

יְהֹוָה עֲשֵׂה לְמַעַן אַהֲרֹן

כִּהֵן בְּאוּרֶיךָ וְתֻמֶּיךָ.

וְחוּסָה עַל יִשְׂרָאֵל עַמֶּךָ:

Hashem, act for the sake of Aharon, the priest who carried Your Urim and Tumim, and have compassion on Yisrael, Your people:

Adonai Aseh Lema'an Zechut

Yosef Asir Tzaddikecha,

Vechusah Al Yisra'el Ammecha:

יְהֹוָה עֲשֵׂה לְמַעַן זְכוּת

יוֹסֵף אָסִיר צַדִּיקֶךָ.

וְחוּסָה עַל יִשְׂרָאֵל עַמֶּךָ:

Hashem, act for the sake of the merit of Yosef, the righteous captive, and have compassion on Yisrael, Your people:

Adonai Aseh Lema'an David

Ne'im Zemiroteicha, Vechusah

Al Yisra'el Ammecha:

יְהֹוָה עֲשֵׂה לְמַעַן דָּוִד
נְעִים זְמִירוֹתֶיךָ. וְחוּסָה
עַל יִשְׂרָאֵל עַמֶּךָ:

Hashem, act for the sake of David, who sang Your pleasant songs, and have compassion on Yisrael, Your people:

Adonai Aseh Lema'an Pinchas

Zach Kine Lishmecha, Vechusah

Al Yisra'el Ammecha:

יְהֹוָה עֲשֵׂה לְמַעַן פִּינְחָס
זַךְ קִנֵּא לִשְׁמֶךָ. וְחוּסָה
עַל יִשְׂרָאֵל עַמֶּךָ:

Hashem, act for the sake of Pinchas, the pure zealot for Your name, and have compassion on Yisrael, Your people:

Adonai Aseh Lema'an Melech

Shlomo Banah Bayit Lishmecha,

Vechusah Al Yisra'el Ammecha:

יְהֹוָה עֲשֵׂה לְמַעַן מֶלֶךְ
שְׁלֹמֹה בָּנָה בַּיִת לִשְׁמֶךָ.
וְחוּסָה עַל יִשְׂרָאֵל עַמֶּךָ:

Hashem, act for the sake of King Shlomo, who built a house for Your name, and have compassion on Yisrael, Your people:

Adonai Aseh Lema'an Harugim

Userufim Al Yichud Kedushat

Shemecha, Vechusah Al Yisra'el

Ammecha:

יְהֹוָה עֲשֵׂה לְמַעַן הֲרוּגִים
וּשְׂרוּפִים עַל יִחוּד קְדֻשַּׁת
שְׁמֶךָ. וְחוּסָה עַל יִשְׂרָאֵל
עַמֶּךָ:

Hashem, act for the sake of those who were killed and burned for the Unity and sanctification of Your holy name, and have compassion on Yisrael, Your people:

Adonai Aseh Lema'an	יְהֹוָה עֲשֵׂה לְמַעַן
Shemecha, Vechusah Al Yisra'el	שְׁמֶךָ. וְחוּסָה עַל יִשְׂרָאֵל
Ammecha:	עַמֶּךָ:

Hashem, act for the sake of Your name, and have compassion on Yisrael, Your people:

Aseh Lema'an

Aseh Lema'an Shemach. Aseh	עֲשֵׂה לְמַעַן שְׁמָךְ. עֲשֵׂה
Lema'an Amitach. Aseh Lema'an	לְמַעַן אֲמִתָּךְ. עֲשֵׂה לְמַעַן
Beritach. Aseh Lema'an	בְּרִיתָךְ. עֲשֵׂה לְמַעַן
Gadelach. Aseh Lema'an	גָּדְלָךְ. עֲשֵׂה לְמַעַן
Datach. Aseh Lema'an	דָּתָךְ. עֲשֵׂה לְמַעַן
Hadarach. Aseh Lema'an	הֲדָרָךְ. עֲשֵׂה לְמַעַן
Vi'udach. Aseh Lema'an	וְיעוּדָךְ. עֲשֵׂה לְמַעַן
Zichrach. Aseh Lema'an	זִכְרָךְ. עֲשֵׂה לְמַעַן
Chasdach. Aseh Lema'an Tuvach.	חַסְדָּךְ. עֲשֵׂה לְמַעַן טוּבָךְ.
Aseh Lema'an Yasherach. Aseh	עֲשֵׂה לְמַעַן יָשְׁרָךְ. עֲשֵׂה
Lema'an Kevodach. Aseh	לְמַעַן כְּבוֹדָךְ. עֲשֵׂה
Lema'an Limudach. Aseh	לְמַעַן לִמּוּדָךְ. עֲשֵׂה
Lema'an Malchutach. Aseh	לְמַעַן מַלְכוּתָךְ. עֲשֵׂה
Lema'an Nitzchach. Aseh	לְמַעַן נִצְחָךְ. עֲשֵׂה
Lema'an Sodach. Aseh Lema'an	לְמַעַן סוֹדָךְ. עֲשֵׂה לְמַעַן
Uzach. Aseh Lema'an Pe'erach.	עֻזָּךְ. עֲשֵׂה לְמַעַן פְּאֵרָךְ.
Aseh Lema'an Tzidkatach. Aseh	עֲשֵׂה לְמַעַן צִדְקָתָךְ. עֲשֵׂה
Lema'an Kedushatach. Aseh	לְמַעַן קְדֻשָּׁתָךְ. עֲשֵׂה
Lema'an Rachamanutach. Aseh	לְמַעַן רַחֲמָנוּתָךְ. עֲשֵׂה

Lema'an Shechinatach. Aseh

Lema'an Toratach:

לְמַעַן שְׁכִינָתָךְ. עֲשֵׂה
לְמַעַן תּוֹרָתָךְ:

Act for the sake of Your name. Act for the sake of Your truth. Act for the sake of Your covenant. Act for the sake of Your greatness. Act for the sake of Your Law. Act for the sake of Your majesty. Act for the sake of Your uniqueness. Act for the sake of Your memory. Act for the sake of Your kindness. Act for the sake of Your goodness. Act for the sake of Your uprightness. Act for the sake of Your glory. Act for the sake of Your teaching. Act for the sake of Your kingdom. Act for the sake of Your eternal name. Act for the sake of Your secret. Act for the sake of Your strength. Act for the sake of Your splendor. Act for the sake of Your justice. Act for the sake of Your holiness. Act for the sake of Your compassion. Act for the sake of Your Divine Presence. Act for the sake of Your Torah.

Aseh Lema'an Avraham Yitzchak

Veya'akov. Aseh Lema'an

Mosheh Ve'aharon. Aseh

Lema'an Yosef David Ushlomo.

Aseh Lema'an Yerushalayim Ir

Hakodesh. Aseh Lema'an Tziyon

Mishkan Kevodach. Aseh

Lema'an Chareban Beitach. Aseh

Lema'an Shimamut Heichalach.

Aseh Lema'an Yisra'el

Ha'aniyim. Aseh Lema'an

Yisra'el Hadallim. Aseh Lema'an

Yisra'el Hasheruyim Betzarot.

Aseh Lema'an Yetomim

עֲשֵׂה לְמַעַן אַבְרָהָם יִצְחָק
וְיַעֲקֹב. עֲשֵׂה לְמַעַן
מֹשֶׁה וְאַהֲרֹן. עֲשֵׂה
לְמַעַן יוֹסֵף דָּוִד וּשְׁלֹמֹה.
עֲשֵׂה לְמַעַן יְרוּשָׁלַיִם עִיר
הַקֹּדֶשׁ. עֲשֵׂה לְמַעַן צִיּוֹן
מִשְׁכַּן כְּבוֹדָךְ. עֲשֵׂה
לְמַעַן חָרְבַּן בֵּיתָךְ. עֲשֵׂה
לְמַעַן שִׁמֲמוּת הֵיכָלָךְ.
עֲשֵׂה לְמַעַן יִשְׂרָאֵל
הָעֲנִיִּים. עֲשֵׂה לְמַעַן
יִשְׂרָאֵל הַדַּלִּים. עֲשֵׂה לְמַעַן
יִשְׂרָאֵל הַשְּׁרוּיִים בְּצָרוֹת.
עֲשֵׂה לְמַעַן יְתוֹמִים

Ve'almanot. Aseh Lema'an	וְאַלְמָנוֹת. עֲשֵׂה לְמַעַן
Yonekei Shadayim. Aseh	יוֹנְקֵי שָׁדַיִם. עֲשֵׂה
Lema'an Gemulei Chalav. Aseh	לְמַעַן גְּמוּלֵי חָלָב. עֲשֵׂה
Lema'an Tinokot Shel Beit	לְמַעַן תִּינוֹקוֹת שֶׁל בֵּית
Rabban Shello Chate'u:	רַבָּן שֶׁלֹּא חָטָאוּ:

Act for the sake of Avraham, Yitzchak, and Yaakov. Act for the sake of Moshe and Aharon. Act for the sake of Yosef, David, and Shlomo. Act for the sake of Yerushalayim, the holy city. Act for the sake of Tziyon, the dwelling of Your glory. Act for the sake of the destruction of Your house. Act for the sake of the desolation of Your temple. Act for the sake of the poor of Yisrael. Act for the sake of the downtrodden of Yisrael. Act for the sake of the Israelites who are in distress. Act for the sake of orphans and widows. Act for the sake of those who suckle at the breast. Act for the sake of those who are weaned from milk. Act for the sake of the young school children who have not sinned.

Aseh Lema'anach Im Lo	עֲשֵׂה לְמַעַנְךָ אִם לֹא
Lema'anenu. Aseh Lema'anach	לְמַעֲנֵנוּ. עֲשֵׂה לְמַעַנְךָ
Vehoshi'enu. Hoshi'enu	וְהוֹשִׁיעֵנוּ. הוֹשִׁיעֵנוּ
Va'anenu Hayom Uvechol Yom	וַעֲנֵנוּ הַיּוֹם וּבְכָל יוֹם
Vayom Bitfillatenu Ki	וְיוֹם בִּתְפִלָּתֵנוּ כִּי
Tehillatenu Attah:	תְהִלָּתֵנוּ אָתָּה:

Act for Your sake, if not for our sake. Act for Your sake and save us. Save us and answer us today and every day with our prayers, for You are our praise.

Continue with De'anei on the next page.

De'anei

De'anei La'aniyei. Aneinan:	דְּעָנֵי לַעֲנִיֵּי. עֲנֵינָן:
De'anei La'ashikei. Aneinan:	דְּעָנֵי לַעֲשִׁיקֵי. עֲנֵינָן:
De'anei Litvirei Liba. Aneinan:	דְּעָנֵי לִתְבִירֵי לִבָּא. עֲנֵינָן:
De'anei Leshiflei Da'ta. Aneinan:	דְּעָנֵי לִשְׁפְלֵי דַעְתָּא. עֲנֵינָן:
De'anei Lemakichei Rucha.	דְּעָנֵי לְמַכִּיכֵי רוּחָא.
Aneinan: De'anei Le'avraham	עֲנֵינָן: דְּעָנֵי לְאַבְרָהָם
Avinu Behar Hamoriyah.	אָבִינוּ בְּהַר הַמּוֹרִיָּה.
Aneinan: De'anei Leyitzchak Al	עֲנֵינָן: דְּעָנֵי לְיִצְחָק עַל
Gabei Madbecha. Aneinan:	גַּבֵּי מַדְבְּחָא. עֲנֵינָן:
De'anei Leya'akov Beveit El.	דְּעָנֵי לְיַעֲקֹב בְּבֵית אֵל.
Aneinan: De'anei Leyosef Beveit	עֲנֵינָן: דְּעָנֵי לְיוֹסֵף בְּבֵית
Asirei. Aneinan: De'anei	אֲסִירֵי. עֲנֵינָן: דְּעָנֵי
Lemosheh Va'avoteinu Al Yam	לְמֹשֶׁה וַאֲבוֹתֵינוּ עַל יַם
Suf. Aneinan: De'anei Le'aharon	סוּף. עֲנֵינָן: דְּעָנֵי לְאַהֲרֹן
Bamachta. Aneinan: De'anei	בַּמַּחְתָּא. עֲנֵינָן: דְּעָנֵי
Lefinchas Bashittim. Aneinan:	לְפִינְחָס בַּשִּׁטִּים. עֲנֵינָן:
De'anei Lihoshua' Baggilgal.	דְּעָנֵי לִיהוֹשֻׁעַ בַּגִּלְגָּל.
Aneinan: De'anei Le'eli	עֲנֵינָן: דְּעָנֵי לְעֵלִי
Baramah. Aneinan: De'anei	בָּרָמָה. עֲנֵינָן: דְּעָנֵי
Lishmu'el Bamitzpah. Aneinan:	לִשְׁמוּאֵל בַּמִּצְפָּה. עֲנֵינָן:
De'anei Ledavid Velishlomo	דְּעָנֵי לְדָוִד וְלִשְׁלֹמֹה
Beno Birushalayim. Aneinan:	בְּנוֹ בִּירוּשָׁלַיִם. עֲנֵינָן:
De'anei Le'eliyahu Behar	דְּעָנֵי לְאֵלִיָּהוּ בְּהַר
Hakarmel. Aneinan: De'anei	הַכַּרְמֶל. עֲנֵינָן: דְּעָנֵי
Le'elisha Biricho. Aneinan:	לֶאֱלִישָׁע בִּירִיחוֹ. עֲנֵינָן:
De'anei Lechizkiyahu Bachaloto.	דְּעָנֵי לְחִזְקִיָּהוּ בַּחֲלוֹתוֹ.

Aneinan: De'anei Leyonah	עֲנֵינָן: דְּעָנֵי לְיוֹנָה
Bim'ei Hadagah. Aneinan:	בִּמְעֵי הַדָּגָה. עֲנֵינָן:
De'anei Lachananyah Misha'el	דְּעָנֵי לַחֲנַנְיָה מִישָׁאֵל
Va'azaryah Bego Attun Nura	וַעֲזַרְיָה בְּגוֹ אַתּוּן נוּרָא
Yakidta. Aneinan: De'anei	יַקְדְּתָּא. עֲנֵינָן: דְּעָנֵי
Ledaniyel Beguba De'aryavata.	לְדָנִיֵּאל בְּגֻבָּא דְאַרְיָוָתָא.
Aneinan: De'anei Lemordechai	עֲנֵינָן: דְּעָנֵי לְמָרְדְּכַי
Ve'ester Beshushan Habirah.	וְאֶסְתֵּר בְּשׁוּשַׁן הַבִּירָה.
Aneinan: De'anei Le'ezra	עֲנֵינָן: דְּעָנֵי לְעֶזְרָא
Baggolah. Aneinan: De'anei	בַּגּוֹלָה. עֲנֵינָן: דְּעָנֵי
Lechoni Bama'gal. Aneinan:	לְחוֹנִי בַּמַּעְגָּל. עֲנֵינָן:
De'anei Letzaddikei Vachasidei	דְּעָנֵי לְצַדִּיקֵי וַחֲסִידֵי
Utemimei Di Bechol Dor Vedor.	וּתְמִימֵי דִּי בְּכָל דָּר וְדָר.
Aneinan: Rachamana Aneinan.	עֲנֵינָן: רַחֲמָנָא עֲנֵינָן.
Rachamana Sheziv. Rachamana	רַחֲמָנָא שְׁזִיב. רַחֲמָנָא
Perok. Rachamana Deyitmelei	פְּרוֹק. רַחֲמָנָא דְּיִתְמְלֵי
Rachamin Rachem Alana Ve'al	רַחֲמִין רַחֵם עֲלָנָא וְעַל
Kol Anshei Veitana. Ve'al Kol	כָּל אַנְשֵׁי בֵיתָנָא. וְעַל כָּל
Yisra'el Achana. Umechashocha	יִשְׂרָאֵל אֲחָנָא. וּמֵחֲשׁוֹכָא
Linhora Apekinan Bedil Shemach	לִנְהוֹרָא אַפְּקִנָן בְּדִיל שְׁמָךְ
Rabba:	רַבָּא:

He Who answers the poor, answer us. He Who answers the oppressed, answer us. He Who answers those who are broken hearted, answer us. He Who answers those of humble understanding, answer us. He Who answers those who are humble of spirit, answer us. He Who answered Avraham our father on Mount Moriah, answer us. He Who answered Yitzchak on the altar, answer us. He Who answered Yaakov in Beit-El, answer us. He Who answered Yosef in prison, answer us. He Who answered Moshe and our forefathers at the Sea of Reeds, answer us. He Who answered Aharon with the firepan, answer us. He Who answered Pinchas at Shittim, answer us. He Who answered Yehoshua at Gilgal, answer us. He Who answered Eli at Ramah, answer us. He Who answered Shemuel at Mizpah, answer us. He Who answered David and Shlomo his son in Yerushalayim, answer us. He Who answered Eliyahu on Mount Carmel, answer us. He Who answered Elisha at Yericho, answer us. He Who answered Chizkiyahu in his illness, answer us. He Who answered Yonah in the belly of the fish, answer us. He Who answered Chananiah, Mishael, and Azariah in the fiery furnace, answer us. He Who answered Daniel in the lions den, answer us. He Who answered Mordecai and Esther in Shushan the capital, answer us. He Who answered Ezra in exile, answer us. He Who answered Honi in the circle, answer us. He Who answers the righteous, the pious, and the sincere in every generation, answer us. Merciful One, answer us. Merciful One, have pity. Merciful One, redeem. Merciful One, Who is full of mercy, have mercy on us and on all the members of our household. And on all Yisrael our brothers. And from darkness to light, lead us through for the sake of the greatness of Your Name.

On the Ten Days of Repentance, some say:

Yah Shema Evyoneicha.	יָהּ שְׁמַע אֶבְיוֹנֶיךָ.
Hamechallim Paneicha. Avinu	הַמְחַלִּים פָּנֶיךָ. אָבִינוּ
Levaneicha. Al Ta'lem	לְבָנֶיךָ. אַל תַּעְלֵם
Azeneicha.	אָזְנֶיךָ.

God, listen to your poor ones seeking Your presence. Our Father, to Your children do not hide Your ear.

Yah Am Mima'amakim. Yikre'u

Merov Metzukim. Al Na

Teshivem Rekim. Hayom

Millefaneicha:

יָהּ עַם מִמַּעֲמַקִּים. יִקְרָאוּ
מֵרֹב מְצוּקִים. אַל נָא
תְּשִׁיבֵם רֵקִים. הַיּוֹם
מִלְּפָנֶיךָ:

God, people who from the depths are calling from great troubles.
Do not send them away empty today from before You.

Havotam Va'avonam. Mecheh

Verubei Zedonam. Ve'im Lo

Ta'aseh Lema'anam. Aseh Tzuri

Lema'anecha:

הַוֹּתָם וַעֲוֹנָם. מְחֵה
וְרֻבֵּי זְדוֹנָם. וְאִם לֹא
תַעֲשֶׂה לְמַעֲנָם. עֲשֵׂה צוּרִי
לְמַעֲנֶךָ:

Their evils and iniquity erase, and their great insolence. But if You
will not do it for their sake; do it, my Rock, for Your sake.

Umecheh Hayom Chovam.

Uretzeh Kemo Shai Nivam.

Ulecha Tachin Libam. Vegam

Takshiv Oznecha:

וּמְחֵה הַיּוֹם חוֹבָם.
וּרְצֵה כְּמוֹ שַׁי נִיבָם.
וּלְךָ תָּכִין לִבָּם. וְגַם
תַּקְשִׁיב אָזְנֶךָ:

And erase their debt today, and accept their utterances like a gift.
And lead their hearts to You; but also let Your ears listen.

Dim'at Peneihem Tish'eh.

Vete'esof Eder To'eh. Vetakim

Lecha Ro'eh. Ufekod Betov

Tzonecha:

דִּמְעַת פְּנֵיהֶם תִּשְׁעֶה.
וְתֶאֱסֹף עֵדֶר תּוֹעֶה. וְתָקִים
לְךָ רוֹעֶה. וּפְקֹד בְּטוֹב
צֹאנֶךָ:

The tears on their faces, answer, and gather the wandering flock.
And establish a shepherd for Yourself, and tend well Your flock.

Holechei Bederech Nechochah.	הוֹלְכֵי בְּדֶרֶךְ נְכוֹחָה.
Tevasheorem Hayom Selichah.	תְּבַשְּׂרֵם הַיּוֹם סְלִיחָה.
Uvitfillat Hashachar. Hamtzi'em	וּבִתְפִלַּת הַשַּׁחַר. הַמְצִיאֵם
Chinecha:	חִנֶּךָ:

Those who walk on a proper path, announce forgiveness today.
And in the morning prayer, offer them Your grace.

Im Afes Rova Haken

Im Afes Rova Haken. Ohel	אִם אָפֵס רֹבַע הַקֵּן. אֹהֶל
Shiken Im Riken. Al Na Novdah	שָׁכֵן אִם רֵקֵן. אַל נָא נֹאבְדָה
Ki Al Ken. Yesh Lanu Av Zaken:	כִּי עַל כֵּן. יֵשׁ לָנוּ אָב זָקֵן:
Panim Lo Takir. Vetzidko	פָּנִים לוֹ תַכִּיר. וְצִדְקוֹ
Lefaneicha Nazkir. Kach Na Ben	לְפָנֶיךָ נַזְכִּיר. קַח נָא בֶן
Yakir. Venimtzah Damo Al Kir:	יַקִּיר. וְנִמְצָה דָמוֹ עַל קִיר:
Ratz El Hana'ar Lehakdisho.	רָץ אֶל הַנַּעַר לְהַקְדִּישׁוֹ.
Venafsho Keshurah Benafsho.	וְנַפְשׁוֹ קְשׁוּרָה בְנַפְשׁוֹ.
Itero Ba'etzim Ve'isho. Nezer	עִטְּרוֹ בָּעֵצִים וְאִשּׁוֹ. נֵזֶר
Elohav Al Rosho: Yachid Hukal	אֱלֹהָיו עַל רֹאשׁוֹ: יָחִיד הוּקַל
Katzevi. Anah Ve'amar Avi.	כַּצְּבִי. עָנָה וְאָמַר אָבִי.
Hineh Ha'esh Veha'etzim Navi.	הִנֵּה הָאֵשׁ וְהָעֵצִים נָבִיא.
Uteshurah Ein Lehavi: Millim	וּתְשׁוּרָה אֵין לְהָבִיא: מִלִּים
Heshivo Millehavhilo. Vaya'an	הֵשִׁיבוֹ מִלְּהַבְהִילוֹ. וַיַּעַן
Vayomer Lo. Beni, Elohim Yir'eh	וַיֹּאמֶר לוֹ. בְּנִי. אֱלֹהִים יִרְאֶה

Lo. Veyoda Adonai Et Asher Lo:	לוֹ. וְיוֹדַע יְהֹוָה אֶת אֲשֶׁר לוֹ:
Bemitzvatecha Sheneihem	בְּמִצְוָתְךָ שְׁנֵיהֶם
Nizharim. Ve'achareicha Lo	נִזְהָרִים. וְאַחֲרֶיךָ לֹא
Meharherim. Chashu Vehalechu	מְהַרְהְרִים. חָשׁוּ וְהָלְכוּ
Nimharim. Al Achad Heharim:	נִמְהָרִים. עַל אַחַד הֶהָרִים:
Ra'u Ed Telulah. Miharu Atzei	רָאוּ אֵד תְּלוּלָה. מִהֲרוּ עֲצֵי
Olah. Yachad Be'ahavah Kelulah.	עוֹלָה. יַחַד בְּאַהֲבָה כְּלוּלָה.
Yasheru Ba'aravah Mesillah:	יַשְּׁרוּ בָּעֲרָבָה מְסִלָּה:
Ra'ah Yachid Ki Hu Hasheoh.	רָאָה יָחִיד כִּי הוּא הַשֶּׂה.
Na'am Lehoro Hamenusseh. Avi	נָאַם לְהוֹרוֹ הַמְנֻסֶּה. אָבִי
Oti Kakeves Ta'ashe. Lo Tachmol	אוֹתִי כַּכֶּבֶשׂ תַּעֲשֶׂה. לֹא תַחְמֹל
Velo Techasseh: Bi Chafetz	וְלֹא תְכַסֶּה: בִּי חָפֵץ
Venichsof. Levavi Lo Lachasof.	וְנִכְסֹף. לְבָבִי לוֹ לַחֲשֹׂף.
Im Timna'eni Sof. Ruchi	אִם תִּמְנָעֵנִי סוֹף. רוּחִי
Venishmati Elav Ye'esof: Yadav	וְנִשְׁמָתִי אֵלָיו יֶאֱסֹף: יָדָיו
Veraglav Akad. Vecharbo Alav	וְרַגְלָיו עָקַד. וְחַרְבּוֹ עָלָיו
Pakad. Lesumo Al Ha'etzim	פָּקַד. לְשׂוּמוֹ עַל הָעֵצִים
Shakad. Veha'esh Al	שָׁקַד. וְהָאֵשׁ עַל
Hamizbeach Tukad: Tzavar	הַמִּזְבֵּחַ תּוּקַד: צַוָּאר
Pashat Me'elav. Ve'aviv Niggash	פָּשַׁט מֵאֵלָיו. וְאָבִיו נִגַּשׁ
Elav. Leshochato Leshem Be'alav.	אֵלָיו. לְשָׁחֲטוֹ לְשֵׁם בְּעָלָיו.
Vehineh Adonai Nitzav Alav:	וְהִנֵּה יְהֹוָה נִצָּב עָלָיו:
Chakor Et Kol Asher Asah. Ha'av	חֲקֹר אֶת כָּל אֲשֶׁר עָשָׂה. הָאָב
Al Beno Lo Chasah. Velibo El	עַל בְּנוֹ לֹא חָסָה. וְלִבּוֹ אֶל
Kapayim Nasa. Vayar Elohim Et	כַּפַּיִם נָשָׂא. וַיַּרְא אֱלֹהִים אֶת
Kol Asher Asah: Kara Merechem	כָּל אֲשֶׁר עָשָׂה: קָרָא מֵרֶחֶם
Mishchar. Temur Bincha	מִשְׁחָר. תְּמוּר בִּנְךָ

Hanivchar. Vehineh Ayil Achar.	הַנִּבְחָר. וְהִנֵּה אַיִל אַחַר.
Va'aseh Al Te'achar: Chalifei	וַעֲשֵׂה אַל תְּאַחַר: חֲלִיפֵי
Azkarato. Tikon Kehaktarato.	אַזְכָּרָתוֹ. תִּכּוֹן כְּהַקְטָרָתוֹ.
Veta'aleh Lecha Timrato.	וְתַעֲלֶה לְךָ תִּימְרָתוֹ.
Vehayah Hu Utemurato:	וְהָיָה הוּא וּתְמוּרָתוֹ:

If the dwelling place is destroyed, the Sanctuary of Your Presence is empty. Please do not let us be lost, for we have an elder father (Avraham). Recognize his face and remember his righteousness before You. Please take the precious son (Yitzchak), and let his blood be found on the (Altar) wall. He ran to the youth to sanctify him, his soul bound with his own soul. Surround him with wood and fire, the crown of his God upon his head. The only son was light as a deer, he spoke and said, "My father, behold, the fire and the wood are brought, but there is no offering to bring." Words brought back to him to not scare him. And he answered and said to him, "My son, God will see for Himself, and Hashem will make known what is His." They were both careful in your commandments and did not hesitate to follow you. They hurried and went quickly to one of the mountains. They saw a heap of ruins, and they hurried to gather the wood for the offering. Together, in complete love, they made a path through the wilderness. The only son saw that he was the lamb. He told his tested father, "My father, make me like a lamb. Do not be merciful and do not conceal." In me, he desired and yearned. My heart was exposed to Him. If You withhold me in the end, my spirit and soul will be gathered to Him. He bound his hands and feet, and he placed his knife upon him. He hastened to put him on the wood, and the fire was kindled upon the altar. He stretched out his own neck, and his father approached him to slaughter him for the sake of his Master. And behold, Hashem stood upon him, considering all that he had done. The father did not take pity on his son and lifted his heart to heaven. God saw all that he had done. He called from the birth of dawn, "Exchange your chosen son. And behold, there was another ram, and do not delay in preparing it. As a memorial for him, set it up as his offering, and let it ascend to You. And let him and his substitute be.

Zikaron Lefaneicha Bashachak.	זִכָּרוֹן לְפָנֶיךָ בַּשַׁחַק.
La'ad Bassefer Yuchak. Berit	לָעַד בַּסֵּפֶר יוּחַק. בְּרִית
Olam Bal Yumchak. Et Avraham	עוֹלָם בַּל יֻמְחַק. אֶת אַבְרָהָם
Ve'et Yitzchak: Kore'eicha Ba'im	וְאֶת יִצְחָק: קוֹרְאֶיךָ בָּאִים
Lakod. Betzarah Akedah	לָקוֹד. בְּצָרָה עֲקֵדָה
Tishkod. Vetzoncha	תִּשְׁקֹד. וְצֹאנְךָ
Berachamim Tifkod. Penei	בְּרַחֲמִים תִּפְקֹד. פְּנֵי
Hatzon El Akod: Orerah	הַצֹּאן אֶל עָקוֹד: עוֹרְרָה
Gevuratecha Lehakitz	גְּבוּרָתְךָ לְהָקִיץ
Nirdamim. Lema'ancha Tifdeh	נִרְדָּמִים. לְמַעַנְךָ תִּפְדֶּה
Charedim Nidhamim.	חֲרֵדִים נִדְהָמִים.
Lehamshich Rachameicha	לְהַמְשִׁיךְ רַחֲמֶיךָ
Vachasadeicha Mishemei	וַחֲסָדֶיךָ מִשְּׁמֵי
Meromim. El Melech Yoshev Al Kisse	מְרוֹמִים. אֵל מֶלֶךְ יוֹשֵׁב עַל כִּסֵּא
Rachamim:	רַחֲמִים:

A remembrance before You in heaven, forever inscribed in the book. An eternal covenant that shall not be erased, with Avraham and Yitzchak. Your callers come to bow, in times of trouble the binding (of Yitzchak) will keep watch. And Your flock, in mercy, You shall visit. The faces of the flock are toward the binding (of Yitzchak). Arouse Your might to awaken the dormant ones. For Your sake, redeem the trembling and astonished ones to draw out Your mercy and loving-kindness from the high heavens. God, King, sitting on the throne of mercy.

The Thirteen Attributes of Mercy

El Melech Yoshev Al Kisse	אֵל מֶלֶךְ יוֹשֵׁב עַל כִּסֵּא
Rachamim Umitnaheg	רַחֲמִים וּמִתְנַהֵג
Bachasidut. Mochel Avonot	בַּחֲסִידוּת. מוֹחֵל עֲוֹנוֹת
Ammo Ma'avir Rishon Rishon.	עַמּוֹ מַעֲבִיר רִאשׁוֹן רִאשׁוֹן.
Marbeh Mechilah Lachata'im.	מַרְבֶּה מְחִילָה לַחַטָּאִים.
Uselichah Laposhe'im. Oseh	וּסְלִיחָה לַפּוֹשְׁעִים. עוֹשֶׂה
Tzedakot Im Kol Basar Veruach.	צְדָקוֹת עִם כָּל בָּשָׂר וְרוּחַ.
Lo Chera'atam Lahem Gomel.	לֹא כְרָעָתָם לָהֶם גּוֹמֵל.
El Horetanu Lomar Midot	אֵל הוֹרֵתָנוּ לוֹמַר מִדּוֹת
Shelosh Esreh. Zechor Lanu	שְׁלֹשׁ עֶשְׂרֵה. זְכָר לָנוּ
Hayom Berit Shelosh Esreh.	הַיּוֹם בְּרִית שְׁלֹשׁ עֶשְׂרֵה.
Kemo Shehoda'ta Le'anav	כְּמוֹ שֶׁהוֹדַעְתָּ לֶעָנָו
Mikedem. Vechen Katuv	מִקֶּדֶם. וְכֵן כָּתוּב
Betoratach. Vayered Adonai	בְּתוֹרָתָךְ. וַיֵּרֶד יְהֹוָה
Be'anan Vayityatzev Imo Sham.	בֶּעָנָן וַיִּתְיַצֵּב עִמּוֹ שָׁם.
Vayikra Veshem, Adonai.	וַיִּקְרָא בְשֵׁם. יְהֹוָה.
Vesham Ne'emar:	וְשָׁם נֶאֱמַר:

Sovereign God, enthroned in mercy, You deal with us tenderly, again pardoning the sins of Your people even though they sin again. You are ever ready to give pardon to sinners and forgiveness to transgressors, acting in charity towards all with breath of life, not requiting them according to the evil they do. You, God, Who has taught us to repeat the thirteen attributes of mercy, remember to us this day the covenant of those attributes, as You revealed them of old to Moshe the humble, in the words written in Your Torah: "And Hashem descended in the cloud, and stood with him there, and proclaimed the name of Hashem." (Exodus 34:5) And there it says:

[*] denotes a slight pause between words:

וַיַּעֲבֹר יְהֹוָה עַל פָּנָיו וַיִּקְרָא. יְהֹוָה * יְהֹוָה אֵל רַחוּם וְחַנּוּן. אֶרֶךְ אַפַּיִם וְרַב חֶסֶד וֶאֱמֶת: נֹצֵר חֶסֶד לָאֲלָפִים נֹשֵׂא עָוֹן וָפֶשַׁע וְחַטָּאָה. וְנַקֵּה: וְסָלַחְתָּ לַעֲוֹנֵנוּ וּלְחַטָּאתֵנוּ וּנְחַלְתָּנוּ:

Vaya'avor Adonai Al Panav Vayikra, Adonai | Adonai El Rachum Vechanun, Erech Apayim Verav Chesed Ve'emet: Notzer Chesed La'alafim Nose Avon Vafesha Vechata'ah, Venakeh: Vesalachta La'avonenu Ulechatatenu Unechaltanu:

And Hashem passed by before him, and proclaimed: 'Hashem * Hashem, God, merciful and gracious, long-suffering, and abundant in goodness and truth; keeping mercy to the thousandth generation, forgiving iniquity and transgression and sin, and clearing (those who repent); and You shall forgive our iniquity and our sin, and take us for Your inheritance.

Some have the custom to say this, other continue to next:

לְמִתְוַדֶּה חַטֹּאתָיו. וּמוֹדֶה עַל רֹב אֲשָׁמָיו. אֲשֶׁר בַּהֶבֶל שְׁנוֹתָיו. כָּלוּ בְיָגוֹן יָמָיו. צוֹעֵק מִצָּרוֹתָיו. וּמִבֵּין תִּגְרַת קָמָיו. נִפְלָה נָא בְיַד יְהֹוָה כִּי רַבִּים רַחֲמָיו: מִהְיוֹתִי מָשְׁכְתִּי. בְּחַבְלֵי הַשָּׁוְא עֲוֹנִי. לָכֵן שַׁבְתִּי וְנִחַמְתִּי. כִּי לֹא אֵדַע יוֹם דִּינִי. וּשְׁאֵרִי הִקְרַבְתִּי. וְנָסַכְתִּי מֵי עֵינִי. אוּלַי יְרַחֵם קוֹנִי. כִּי לֹא כָלוּ רַחֲמָיו: נִפְלָה נָא בְיַד יְהֹוָה כִּי רַבִּים רַחֲמָיו: שָׁדַי גִּילִי צָמְקוּ. וְאֵינַק רֹאשׁ פְּתָנִים. וּמֵי עֵינַי שָׁחֲקוּ. מֵעוֹז כְּאֵבִי אֲבָנִים. וְרַחֲמֵי אָב רָחָקוּ. וְלֹא חָמַל עַל בָּנִים. וְאֵלַי יִתְאַפָּקוּ. הֲמוֹן מֵעָיו וְרַחֲמָיו: נִפְלָה נָא בְיַד יְהֹוָה כִּי רַבִּים רַחֲמָיו: הֱבִיאָנִי בְּבוֹר לָבָאִים. וְהִנְחִילַנִי קֶצְפּוֹ. וְנִשְׁכַּחְתִּי בְּבֵית כְּלָאִים. וְטָבַעְתִּי בְיָם זַעְפּוֹ. בְּכָל יוֹם יָרַדְתִּי פְלָאִים. אַחֲרֵי הֶאֱרִיךְ לִי אַפּוֹ. הֲשָׁכַח חַנּוֹת אֵל. אִם קָפַץ בְּאַף רַחֲמָיו: נִפְלָה נָא בְיַד יְהֹוָה כִּי רַבִּים רַחֲמָיו:

Lemitvadeh Chatotav. Umodeh Al Rov Ashamav. Asher Bahevel Shenotav. Kalu Veyagon Yamav. Tzo'ek Mitzarotav. Umibein Tigrat Kamav. Nipelah Na Beyad Adonai Ki Rabbim Rachamav: Mihyoti Mashachti. Bechavlei Hashave Avoni. Lachen Shavti Venichamti. Ki Lo Eda Yom Dini. Ushe'eri Hikravti. Venasachti Mei Eini. Ulai Yerachem Koni. Ki Lo Chalu Rachamav: Nipelah Na Beyad Adonai Ki Rabbim Rachamav: Shedei Gili Tzamaku. Va'inak Rosh Petanim. Umei Einai Shachaku. Me'oz Ke'evi Avanim. Verachamei Av Rachaku. Velo Chamal Al Banim. Ve'elai Yit'apaku. Hamon Me'av Verachamav: Nipelah Na Beyad Adonai Ki Rabbim Rachamav: Hevi'ani Bevor Leva'im. Vehinchilani Kitzpo. Venishkachti Beveit Kela'im. Vetava'ti Beyam Za'po. Bechol Yom Yaradti Pela'im. Acharei He'erich Li Appo. Hashachach Chanot El. Im Kafatz Be'af Rachamav: Nipelah Na Beyad Adonai Ki Rabbim Rachamav:

To confess his sins. And admits to his many guilt. That in the vanity of his years, his days are filled with sorrow. Crying out from his troubles, and understanding the challenge of his enemies. Let me fall into the hands of Hashem, for His mercies are many: from my existence, I was drawn into the ropes of vanity, my sin. Therefore I repented and was comforted, for I do not know the day of my judgment. And the rest I have offered, and I have poured out the waters of my eyes. Perhaps my Maker will have mercy, for his mercies are not exhausted: let me fall into the hands of Hashem, for His mercies are many: my breastfeeding breasts have dried up, and I sucked the top of my thumbs. And the waters of my eyes have turned to dust, from the strength of my sorrow I have been hardened. And the mercy of a father has been removed, and has not had mercy on the children. And to me, let His multitude of insides and mercies be restrained: let me fall into the hands of Hashem, for His mercies are many: He brought me into a pit of lions, and I inherited His wrath. And I was forgotten in a house of prisoners, and I sunk into the sea of His anger. Every day I descended into wonders, after He has prolonged His anger. Has God forgotten to be gracious, or has He shut off His mercies in anger: let me fall into the hands of the Hashem, for His mercies are many.

Some have the custom to say this instead of the previous: Siman Bilam Chazak:

Bezacheri Al Mishkavi, Zedon	בְּזָכְרִי עַל מִשְׁכָּבִי. זָדוֹן
Libi Va'ashamav. Akumah	לִבִּי וַאֲשָׁמָיו. אָקוּמָה
Ve'avo'ah, El Beit Elohai	וְאָבוֹאָה. אֶל בֵּית אֱלֹהַי
Vahadomav. Va'omar Benase'i	וַהֲדוֹמָיו. וְאֹמַר בְּנָשְׂאִי
Ayin, Betachanunai Elei	עַיִן. בְּתַחֲנוּנַי אֱלֵי
Shamav. Nipelah Na Beyad	שָׁמָיו. נִפְּלָה נָא בְּיַד
Adonai Ki Rabbim Rachamav:	יְהֹוָה כִּי רַבִּים רַחֲמָיו:

In my thoughts as I lie down, my heart is full of guilt and sin. I shall rise and go to the house of my God and the silent ones. I will say in lifting my eyes, in my supplication to the heavens: "May I fall into the hand of Hashem, for His mercies are abundant."

Lecha Eli Tzur Cheili, Menusati	לְךָ אֵלִי צוּר חֵילִי. מְנוּסָתִי
Betzarati. Becha Sivri Vetikvati,	בְּצָרָתִי. בְּךָ שִׂבְרִי וְתִקְוָתִי.
Eyaluti Begaluti. Lecha Kol	אֱיָלוּתִי בְּגָלוּתִי. לְךָ כָּל
Mish'alot Libi, Venegdecha Kol	מִשְׁאֲלוֹת לִבִּי. וְנֶגְדְּךָ כָּל
Ta'avati. Pedeh Eved Lecha	תַּאֲוָתִי. פְּדֵה עֶבֶד לְךָ צוֹעֵק.
Tzo'ek, Miyad Rodav Vekamav:	מִיַּד רוֹדָיו וְקָמָיו:

To You, my God, my rock and my refuge in my distress; my hope and my strength, my youth in my exile. To You are all the desires of my heart, and before You are all my cravings. Redeem Your servant who cries out to You, from the hand of his oppressors and adversaries.

Aneni Adonai Aneni, Bekare'i	עֲנֵנִי יְהֹוָה עֲנֵנִי. בְּקָרְאִי מִן
Min Hametzar. Veyivada	הַמֶּצַר. וְיִוָּדַע
Ba'ammim, Ki Yadecha Lo	בָּעַמִּים. כִּי יָדְךָ לֹא
Tiktzar. Ve'al Tivzeh Enut Ani,	תִקְצַר. וְאַל תִּבְזֶה עֱנוּת עָנִי.

Tzo'ek Mitigrat Tzar. Asher צוֹעֵק מִתִּגְרַת צָר. אֲשֶׁר

Pesha'av Lecha Modeh, פְּשָׁעָיו לְךָ מוֹדֶה.

Umitvadeh Al Alumav: וּמִתְוַדֶּה עַל עֲלוּמָיו:

Answer me, Hashem, answer me when I call from distress. Let it be known among the nations that Your hand is not short. Do not despise the humble supplication of the needy, crying out from the bitterness of their distress. He who confesses his transgressions to You, and admits his hidden sins:

Mah Yit'onen Veyomar, Mah מַה יִּתְאוֹנֵן וְיֹאמַר. מַה

Yedaber Veyitztaddak. Yetzir יְדַבֵּר וְיִצְטַדָּק. יְצִיר

Chomer Asher Tashuv, Geviyato חֹמֶר אֲשֶׁר תָּשׁוּב. גְּוִיָּתוֹ

Ke'avak Dak. Mah Yiten Lecha כְּאָבָק דַּק. מַה יִּתֶּן לְךָ

Ha'adam, Ki Yirsha Vechi הָאָדָם. כִּי יִרְשַׁע וְכִי

Yitzdak. Halo Millav Umif'alav, יִצְדָּק. הֲלֹא מִלָּיו וּמִפְעָלָיו.

Ketuvim Besefer Yamav: כְּתוּבִים בְּסֵפֶר יָמָיו:

What can he complain and say, what can he speak and justify himself? A creation of clay that will return, his essence like fine dust. What can a man give to You, whether he sins or is righteous? Are not his words and deeds written in the book of his days?

Chatzot (Na O Be'od) Layelah חֲצוֹת (נ"א בְּעוֹד) לַיְלָה

Lecha Kamu, Avadeicha לְךָ קָמוּ. עֲבָדֶיךָ

Bemahalalam. Zechut Avot בְּמַהֲלָלָם. זְכוּת אָבוֹת

Lahem Tizkor, Ve'al Tefen לָהֶם תִּזְכֹּר. וְאַל תֵּפֶן

Lema'alalam. Keneh Adatecha לְמַעֲלָלָם. קְנֵה עֲדָתְךָ

Kimei Kedem, Kedosh Ya'akov כִּימֵי קֶדֶם. קְדוֹשׁ יַעֲקֹב

Go'alam. Vehinase Ha'el, Oseh גְּאָלָם. וְהִנָּשֵׂא הָאֵל. עוֹשֶׂה

Hashalom Bimromav: הַשָּׁלוֹם בִּמְרוֹמָיו:

At mid- (or while still) night, your servants rise for You, in their praises. Remember the merit of the forefathers for them, and do not turn to their misdeeds. Acquire your congregation as in ancient days, the Holy One of Yaakov their redeemer. And may the exalted God, who makes peace in His heights:

Rachum Vechanun Chatanu   רַחוּם וְחַנּוּן חָטָאנוּ

Lefaneicha Rachem Aleinu   לְפָנֶיךָ רַחֵם עָלֵינוּ

Vehoshi'enu: וְהוֹשִׁיעֵנוּ:

Compassionate and gracious One, we have sinned before You; have mercy upon us and save us.

Psalms 25

לְדָוִד אֵלֶיךָ יְהֹוָה נַפְשִׁי אֶשָּׂא: אֱלֹהַי בְּךָ בָטַחְתִּי אַל אֵבוֹשָׁה. אַל יַעַלְצוּ אוֹיְבַי לִי: גַּם כָּל קֹוֶיךָ לֹא יֵבשׁוּ. יֵבשׁוּ הַבּוֹגְדִים רֵיקָם: דְּרָכֶיךָ יְהֹוָה הוֹדִיעֵנִי. אֹרְחוֹתֶיךָ לַמְּדֵנִי: הַדְרִיכֵנִי בַאֲמִתֶּךָ. וְלַמְּדֵנִי כִּי אַתָּה אֱלֹהֵי יִשְׁעִי. אוֹתְךָ קִוִּיתִי כָּל הַיּוֹם: זְכֹר רַחֲמֶיךָ יְהֹוָה וַחֲסָדֶיךָ. כִּי מֵעוֹלָם הֵמָּה: חַטֹּאת נְעוּרַי וּפְשָׁעַי אַל תִּזְכֹּר. כְּחַסְדְּךָ זְכָר לִי אַתָּה. לְמַעַן טוּבְךָ יְהֹוָה: טוֹב וְיָשָׁר יְהֹוָה. עַל כֵּן יוֹרֶה חַטָּאִים בַּדָּרֶךְ: יַדְרֵךְ עֲנָוִים בַּמִּשְׁפָּט. וִילַמֵּד עֲנָוִים דַּרְכּוֹ: כָּל אָרְחוֹת יְהֹוָה חֶסֶד וֶאֱמֶת. לְנֹצְרֵי בְרִיתוֹ וְעֵדֹתָיו: לְמַעַן שִׁמְךָ יְהֹוָה. וְסָלַחְתָּ לַעֲוֺנִי כִּי רַב הוּא: מִי זֶה הָאִישׁ יְרֵא יְהֹוָה. יוֹרֶנּוּ בְּדֶרֶךְ יִבְחָר: נַפְשׁוֹ בְּטוֹב תָּלִין. וְזַרְעוֹ יִירַשׁ אָרֶץ: סוֹד יְהֹוָה לִירֵאָיו. וּבְרִיתוֹ לְהוֹדִיעָם: עֵינַי תָּמִיד אֶל יְהֹוָה. כִּי הוּא יוֹצִיא מֵרֶשֶׁת רַגְלָי: פְּנֵה אֵלַי וְחָנֵּנִי. כִּי יָחִיד וְעָנִי אָנִי: צָרוֹת לְבָבִי הִרְחִיבוּ. מִמְּצוּקוֹתַי הוֹצִיאֵנִי: רְאֵה עָנְיִי וַעֲמָלִי. וְשָׂא לְכָל חַטֹּאתָי: רְאֵה אֹיְבַי כִּי רָבּוּ.

לְדָוִד אֵלֶיךָ יְהֹוָה נַפְשִׁי אֶשָּׂא: אֱלֹהַי בְּךָ בָטַחְתִּי
אַל אֵבוֹשָׁה אַל יַעַלְצוּ אֹיְבַי לִי: גַּם כָּל קֹוֶיךָ לֹא יֵבֹשׁוּ
יֵבֹשׁוּ הַבּוֹגְדִים רֵיקָם: דְּרָכֶיךָ יְהֹוָה הוֹדִיעֵנִי:
אֹרְחוֹתֶיךָ לַמְּדֵנִי: הַדְרִיכֵנִי בַאֲמִתֶּךָ וְלַמְּדֵנִי כִּי
אַתָּה אֱלֹהֵי יִשְׁעִי:

Ledavid Eleicha Adonai Nafshi Eshao: Elohai Becha Vatachti Al
Evoshah. Al Ya'altzu Oyevai Li: Gam Kol Koveicha Lo Yevoshu.
Yevoshu Habogedim Reikam: Deracheicha Adonai Hodi'eni.
Orechoteicha Lamedeni: Hadricheni Ba'amitecha, Velamedeni Ki
Attah Elohei Yish'i. Otecha Kiviti Kol Hayom: Zechor Rachameicha
Adonai Vachasadeicha. Ki Me'olam Hemah: Chatot Ne'urai
Ufesha'ai Al Tizkor. Kechasdecha Zechar Li Attah. Lema'an Tuvecha
Adonai: Tov Veyashar Adonai. Al Ken Yoreh Chata'im Baddarech:
Yadrech Anavim Bamishpat. Vilamed Anavim Darko: Kol Arechot
Adonai Chesed Ve'emet. Lenotzerei Verito Ve'edotav: Lema'an
Shimcha Adonai. Vesalachta La'avoni Ki Rav Hu: Mi Zeh Ha'ish Yere
Adonai. Yorenu Bederech Yivchar: Nafsho Betov Talin. Vezar'o Yirash
Aretz: Sod Adonai Lire'av. Uverito Lehodi'am: Einai Tamid El
Adonai. Ki Hu Yotzi Mereshet Raglai: Peneh Elai Vechaneni. Ki
Yachid Ve'ani Ani: Tzarot Levavi Hirchivu. Mimetzukotai Hotzi'eni:
Re'eh Aneyi Va'amali. Vesa Lechol Chatotai: Re'eh Oyevai Ki Rabu.
Vesin'at Chamas Sene'uni: Shamerah Nafshi Vehatzileni. Al Evosh Ki
Chasiti Vach: Tom Vayosher Yitzeruni. Ki Kiviticha: Pedeh Elohim Et
Yisra'el. Mikol Tzarotav: Vehu Yifdeh Et Yisra'el. Mikol Avonotav:
Adonai Elohei Yisra'el Shuv Mecharon Apecha. Vehinachem Al
Hara'ah Le'ammecha:

Of David, to You, Hashem, I lift up my soul: My God, in You I trust,
let me not be put to shame; let not my enemies exult over me.
Indeed, let none who wait for You be put to shame; let those be
ashamed that deal treacherously without cause. Make me know
Your ways, Hashem; teach me Your paths. Lead me in Your truth,
and teach me, for You are the God of my salvation; for You I wait all
day long. Remember, Hashem: Your tender mercies and Your
steadfast love, for they have been from of old. Do not remember the
sins of my youth or my transgressions; according to Your steadfast
love remember me, for the sake of Your goodness, Hashem. Good
and upright is Hashem; therefore He instructs sinners in the way. He

leads the humble in what is right, and teaches the humble His way. All the paths of Hashem are steadfast love and faithfulness, for those who keep His covenant and His testimonies. For Your name's sake, Hashem, pardon my guilt, for it is great. What man is he who fears Hashem? He will instruct him in the way that he should choose. His soul shall abide in well-being, and his offspring shall inherit the land. The counsel of Hashem is for those who fear Him, and He makes known to them His covenant. My eyes are ever toward Hashem, for He will pluck my feet out of the net. Turn to me and be gracious to me, for I am lonely and afflicted. The troubles of my heart are enlarged; bring me out of my distresses. Consider my affliction and my trouble, and forgive all my sins. Consider how many are my foes, and with what violent hatred they hate me. Guard my soul, and deliver me. Let me not be put to shame, for I take refuge in You. May integrity and uprightness preserve me, for I wait for You. Redeem Yisrael, God, out of all his troubles. And He will redeem Yisrael from all his iniquities. Hashem, God of Yisrael, Turn back from Your fierce anger, and console us for the evil done to Your people. (Ps. 130:8, Ex: 32:12)

Continue on the next page with the Weekday Techinot.

Weekday Techinot

On the different days of the week add the techinah:

Techinah for Sunday (Siman Shemuel Chazak):

Adonai Shav'at Ammecha	יְהֹוָה שַׁוְעַת עַמְּךָ
Hakshivah. Va'aseh Imanu Ot	הַקְשִׁיבָה. וַעֲשֵׂה עִמָּנוּ אוֹת
Letovah. Umi Ke'ammecha	לְטוֹבָה. וּמִי כְעַמְּךָ
Yisra'el Goy Echad: Mibein	יִשְׂרָאֵל גּוֹי אֶחָד: מִבֵּין
Shinei Arayot Techalletzem.	שְׁנֵי אֲרָיוֹת תְּחַלְּצֵם.
Ume'arba Ruchot Tekabetzem.	וּמֵאַרְבַּע רוּחוֹת תְּקַבְּצֵם.
Vekarev Otam Echad El	וְקָרֵב אוֹתָם אֶחָד אֶל
Echad: Ve'et Avelei Tziyon	אֶחָד: וְאֶת אֲבֵלֵי צִיּוֹן
Tenachem. Ve'et Oholivah	תְּנַחֵם. וְאֶת אָהֳלִיבָה
Hanedudah Terachem. Lechaber	הַנְּדוּדָה תְּרַחֵם. לְחַבֵּר
Et Ha'ohel Lihyot Echad: Edom	אֶת הָאֹהֶל לִהְיוֹת אֶחָד: אֱדוֹם
U'moav Tzametu Babor Chayai.	וּמוֹאָב צָמְתוּ בַּבּוֹר חַיָּי.
Becherpah Hiku Lechayai. Mizeh	בְּחֶרְפָּה הִכּוּ לְחַיָּי.
Echad Umizeh Echad: Leraglai	מִזֶּה אֶחָד וּמִזֶּה אֶחָד: לְרַגְלַי
Tamenu Pach Vafachat.	טָמְנוּ פַח וָפָחַת.
Vayitlachashu Alai Yachad. Ein	וַיִּתְלַחֲשׁוּ עָלַי יַחַד. אֵין
Oseh Tov Ein Gam	עוֹשֵׂה טוֹב אֵין גַּם
Echad: Chazek Ammecha	אֶחָד: חַזֵּק עַמְּךָ
Shochen Shemei Eretz.	שׁוֹכֵן שְׁמֵי אֶרֶץ.
Veoyveicha Yihyu Lechalah	וְאוֹיְבֶיךָ יִהְיוּ לְכָלָה
Vacheretz. Vehayah Adonai	וָחֶרֶץ. וְהָיָה יְהֹוָה
Lemelech Al Kol Ha'aretz.	לְמֶלֶךְ עַל כָּל הָאָרֶץ.
Bayom Hahu Yihyeh Adonai	בַּיּוֹם הַהוּא יִהְיֶה יְהֹוָה
Echad Ushemo Echad: Shuv	אֶחָד וּשְׁמוֹ אֶחָד: שׁוּב

Mecharon Apecha, Vehinachem   מֵחֲרוֹן אַפֶּךָ. וְהִנָּחֵם

Al Hara'ah Le'ammecha: עַל הָרָעָה לְעַמֶּךְ:

Hashem, hear the cry of Your people, perform a sign for our good. And who is like Your people Yisrael, a single nation: Deliver them from between two lions, gather them from the four winds, bring them together, one to another: Comfort the mourners of Tziyon, have mercy on your wandering beloved, to connect the tent to be one: Edom and Moav thirst in the pit of my life, they struck my cheek in shame, from this one and that one: They hid a trap and a pit for my feet, and they whispered against me together. There is no one who does good, not even one: Strengthen your people, Dweller of heaven and earth, and let your enemies become waste and destruction. And Hashem will be king over all the earth. On that day Hashem will be one and His name one: Turn back from Your fierce anger, and console us for the evil done to Your people.

Techinah for Monday (Siman Yehudah Chazak):

Adonai Yachid Libot Kol Benei	יְהֹוָה יָחִיד לִבּוֹת כָּל בְּנֵי
Adam Choker. Oseh Gedolot Ad	אָדָם חוֹקֵר. עוֹשֶׂה גְּדוֹלוֹת עַד
Ein Cheker. Vayhi Erev Vayhi	אֵין חֵקֶר. וַיְהִי עֶרֶב וַיְהִי
Voker Yom Sheni: Hakshev	בֹקֶר יוֹם שֵׁנִי: הַקְשֵׁב
Sichat Avdecha Veni'umo. Sovel	שִׂיחַת עַבְדְּךָ וְנִאֲמוֹ. סוֹבֵל
Galut Al Shichmo. Veyom Noflo	גָּלוּת עַל שִׁכְמוֹ. וְיוֹם נָפְלוֹ
Lahakimo. Yesh Echad Ve'ein	לַהֲקִימוֹ. יֵשׁ אֶחָד וְאֵין
Sheni: Uzechor Berit Yedideicha.	שֵׁנִי: וּזְכֹר בְּרִית יְדִידֶיךָ.
Le'am Tzo'akim Negdecha.	לְעַם צוֹעֲקִים נֶגְדֶּךָ.
Benei Ya'akov Avadeicha.	בְּנֵי יַעֲקֹב עֲבָדֶיךָ.
Vaytzav Gam Et Hasheni: Dodi	וַיְצַו גַּם אֶת הַשֵּׁנִי: דּוֹדִי

Hakshev Techinot. Vachashov	הַקְשֵׁב תְּחִנּוֹת. וַחֲשֹׁב
Tefillotam Kemanot. Bizchut	תְּפִלּוֹתָם כְּמָנוֹת. בִּזְכוּת
Makrivim Korbanot. Netan'el	מַקְרִיבִים קָרְבָּנוֹת. נְתַנְאֵל
Ben Tzu'ar Bayom Hasheni: Hat	בֶּן צוּעָר בַּיּוֹם הַשֵּׁנִי: הַט
Oznecha Litfillat Ammecha.	אָזְנְךָ לִתְפִלַּת עַמֶּךָ.
Ushelach Lanu Meshich	וּשְׁלַח לָנוּ מְשִׁיחַ
Tzidkecha. Venakriv Korebanot	צִדְקֶךָ. וְנַקְרִיב קָרְבָּנוֹת
Lefaneicha. Et Hakeves Echad	לְפָנֶיךָ. אֶת הַכֶּבֶשׂ אֶחָד
Baboker Ve'et Hakeves	בַּבֹּקֶר וְאֶת הַכֶּבֶשׂ
Hasheni: Chazek Libi Malki.	הַשֵּׁנִי: חַזֵּק לִבִּי מַלְכִּי.
Umaher Leha'ir Cheshki. Im	וּמַהֵר לְהָאִיר חֶשְׁכִּי. אִם
Nisterah Darki. Hatzlichah Na	נִסְתְּרָה דַרְכִּי. הַצְלִיחָה נָא
Le'avdecha Bayom	לְעַבְדְּךָ בַּיּוֹם
Hasheni: Shuv Mecharon	הַשֵּׁנִי: שׁוּב מֵחֲרוֹן
Apecha, Vehinachem Al Hara'ah	אַפֶּךָ, וְהִנָּחֵם עַל הָרָעָה
Le'ammecha:	לְעַמֶּךָ:

Hashem, You alone examine all human hearts. You perform great deeds beyond investigation. And there was evening, and there was morning, a second day: Listen to the plea of Your servant, and his utterance. Enduring exile on his shoulder. And the day he fell, to raise him up. There is one and there is no second: Remember the covenant of Your beloved for the people crying out before You. Your servants, the sons of Yaakov. And He also commanded the second: My beloved, heed the supplications, and consider their prayers as offerings. In the merit of those offering sacrifices. Natanel son of Tzuar on the second day: Incline Your ear to the prayer of Your people. And send us Your righteous Messiah. And we will offer sacrifices before You. The one lamb in the morning and the second lamb: Strengthen my heart, my King, and hurry to illuminate my darkness. If my path is hidden, please make it successful for Your servant on the second day: Turn back from Your fierce anger, and console us for the evil done to Your people.

Techinah for Tuesday (Siman David bar Elazar):

Adonai Dallu Einai Lamarom.	יְהֹוָה דַּלּוּ עֵינַי לַמָּרוֹם.
Batzar Li Ekra Adonai: Vattit'attef	בַּצַּר לִי אֶקְרָא יְהֹוָה: וַתִּתְעַטֵּף
Alai Ruchi. Merov Ka'si Vesichi.	עָלַי רוּחִי. מֵרֹב כַּעְסִי וְשִׂיחִי.
Va'eshpoch Et Nafshi Lifnei	וָאֶשְׁפֹּךְ אֶת נַפְשִׁי לִפְנֵי
Adonai: Yah Hakshev Ni'umi.	יְהֹוָה: יָהּ הַקְשֵׁב נְאֻמִי.
Va'aseh Ot Letovah Imi. Rabbot	וַעֲשֵׂה אוֹת לְטוֹבָה עִמִּי. רַבּוֹת
Asita Attah Adonai: Dalloti Veli	עָשִׂיתָ אַתָּה יְהֹוָה: דַּלּוֹתִי וְלִי
Yehoshia'. El Tzaddik Umoshia'.	יְהוֹשִׁיעַ. אֵל צַדִּיק וּמוֹשִׁיעַ.
Lishu'atecha Kiviti	לִישׁוּעָתְךָ קִוִּיתִי
Adonai: Bekum Alai Oyevi. Lo	יְהֹוָה: בְּקוּם עָלַי אוֹיְבִי. לֹא
Yira Libi. Va'ani Aleicha Batachti	יִירָא לִבִּי. וַאֲנִי עָלֶיךָ בָּטַחְתִּי
Adonai: Ramah Becha Yadi	יְהֹוָה: רָמָה בְּךָ יָדִי
Misgabi. Velo Vecharbi. Ki Lo	מִשְׂגַּבִּי. וְלֹא בְחַרְבִּי. כִּי לֹא
Vecherev Uvachanit Yoshia'	בְחֶרֶב וּבַחֲנִית יוֹשִׁיעַ
Adonai: Oyevai Gavaru. Ve'alai	יְהֹוָה: אוֹיְבַי גָּבְרוּ. וְעָלַי
Hit'ammaru. Ha'al Elleh Tit'apak	הִתְאַמְּרוּ. הַעַל אֵלֶּה תִתְאַפַּק
Adonai: Lamah Faneicha Tastir.	יְהֹוָה: לָמָה פָנֶיךָ תַסְתִּיר.
Ve'oyev Alai Yachtir. El Kano	וְאוֹיֵב עָלַי יַכְתִּיר. אֵל קַנּוֹא
Venokem Adonai: Etzot Benafshi	וְנוֹקֵם יְהֹוָה: עֵצוֹת בְּנַפְשִׁי
Asimah. Ve'im Levavi Ahimah.	אָשִׂימָה. וְעִם לְבָבִי אֲהִימָה.
Hal'olamim Yiznach	הַלְעוֹלָמִים יִזְנַח
Adonai: Zedim Yerivuni. Se'ifai	יְהֹוָה: זֵדִים יְרִיבוּנִי. סְעִפַּי

Yeshivuni. Ki Lo Yiznach Le'olam	יְשִׁיבוּנִי. כִּי לֹא יִזְנַח לְעוֹלָם
Adonai: Rachameicha Sibarti. Ki	יְהֹוָה: רַחֲמֶיךָ שִׂבַּרְתִּי. כִּי
Lecha Adonai Hochalti. Attah	לְךָ יְהֹוָה הוֹחַלְתִּי. אַתָּה
Ta'aneh Adonai Elohai: Shuv	תַעֲנֶה יְהֹוָה אֱלֹהָי: שׁוּב
Mecharon Apecha, Vehinachem	מֵחֲרוֹן אַפֶּךָ. וְהִנָּחֵם
Al Hara'ah Le'ammecha:	עַל הָרָעָה לְעַמֶּךָ:

Hashem, my eyes look up to the heights. In distress I call upon Hashem: And my spirit was wrapped about me from my great anger and complaint. And I poured out my soul before Hashem: God, listen to my speech and do a sign for good with me. You have done much, Hashem: My poverty, and save me. A righteous God and savior. For Your salvation I have hoped, Hashem: When my enemy rises against me, my heart will not fear. And I trusted in You, Hashem: I have lifted up my hand to You, my Stronghold. And not by my sword. For not by sword and spear does Hashem save: My enemies have become strong. And they were insolent towards me. On these, will you hold back, Hashem? Why do You hide Your face? And my enemy is abundantly against me. God is jealous and avenges, Hashem: I will make plans in my soul. And with my heart I will be astounded. Will Hashem reject forever? The arrogant contend with me. My lips will answer them. For Hashem will not reject forever: I have hoped for Your mercy. For I have waited for You, Hashem. You will answer, Hashem Elohim: Turn back from Your fierce anger, and console us for the evil done to Your people.

Techinah for Wednesday (Siman Ani David Katan):

Adonai Im Gadal Avoni Mineso.	יְהֹוָה אִם גָּדַל עֲוֹנִי מִנְּשׂוֹא.
Vehiskalti Asoh. Al Tavo	וְהִסְכַּלְתִּי עָשֹׂה. אַל תָּבוֹא
Vemishpat Et Avdecha: Nig'ei	בְמִשְׁפָּט אֶת עַבְדֶּךָ: נִגְעֵי
Levavi Haver. Vechatot Ne'urai	לְבָבִי הָבֵר. וְחַטֹּאת נְעוּרַי

Ha'aver. Gam Mizedim Chasoch	הַעֲבֵר. גַּם מִזֵּדִים חֲשֹׁךְ
Avdecha: Yegonotai Gaveru.	עַבְדֶּךָ: יְגוֹנוֹתַי גָּבְרוּ.
Ve'anchotai Libi Shaveru.	וְאַנְחוֹתַי לִבִּי שָׁבְרוּ.
Sameach Nefesh	שַׂמֵּחַ נֶפֶשׁ
Avdecha: Doreshei Ra'ati Alai	עַבְדֶּךָ: דּוֹרְשֵׁי רָעָתִי עָלַי
Higdilu. Lehavati Yagilu. Al Taster	הִגְדִּילוּ. לְהַוָּתִי יָגִילוּ. אַל תַּסְתֵּר
Paneicha Me'avdecha: Ve'ad An	פָּנֶיךָ מֵעַבְדֶּךָ: וְעַד אָן
Ashavea' Ve'ein Mishpat. Matai	אֲשַׁוֵּעַ וְאֵין מִשְׁפָּט. מָתַי
Ta'aseh Verodefai Mishpat.	תַעֲשֶׂה בְרוֹדְפַי מִשְׁפָּט.
Kamah Yemei Avdecha: Yashuv	כַּמָּה יְמֵי עַבְדֶּךָ: יָשׁוּב
Apecha Lerachameni. Yehi Na	אַפְּךָ לְרַחֲמֵנִי. יְהִי נָא
Chasdecha Lenachameni.	חַסְדְּךָ לְנַחֲמֵנִי.
Ke'imratecha	כְּאִמְרָתֶךָ
Le'avdecha: Derachai Siparti.	לְעַבְדֶּךָ: דְּרָכַי סִפַּרְתִּי.
Ve'aleicha Mibeten Nismachti.	וְעָלֶיךָ מִבֶּטֶן נִסְמַכְתִּי.
Ha'irah Faneicha Al	הָאִירָה פָנֶיךָ עַל
Avdecha: Katoneti Mikol	עַבְדֶּךָ: קָטֹנְתִּי מִכָּל
Hachasadim. Tzur Moshiv	הַחֲסָדִים. צוּר מוֹשִׁיב
Yechidim. Asher Asita Et	יְחִידִים. אֲשֶׁר עָשִׂיתָ אֶת
Avdecha: Tahareni Mechatati. Al	עַבְדֶּךָ: טַהֲרֵנִי מֵחַטָּאתִי. אַל
Ta'lem Oznecha Leravchati	תַעְלֵם אָזְנְךָ לְרַוְחָתִי
Leshav'ati. Ana Adonai Ki Ani	לְשַׁוְעָתִי. אָנָּא יְהוָה כִּי אֲנִי
Avdecha: Nifla'ot Har'eni. Al	עַבְדֶּךָ: נִפְלָאוֹת הַרְאֵנִי. אַל
Taster Paneicha Mimeni. Al Tat	תַּסְתֵּר פָּנֶיךָ מִמֶּנִּי. אַל תֵּט
Be'af Avdecha: Shuv Mecharon	בְּאַף עַבְדֶּךָ: שׁוּב מֵחֲרוֹן
Apecha, Vehinachem Al Hara'ah	אַפֶּךָ. וְהִנָּחֵם עַל הָרָעָה
Le'ammecha:	לְעַמֶּךָ:

Hashem, if my sin is too great to bear. And I have acted foolishly. Do not judge Your servant: Heal the afflictions of my heart. And pass over the sin of my youth. Also, from willful sins, restrain Your servant: My sorrows have grown. And my sighs have broken my heart. Make the soul of Your servant joyful: Those seeking my harm have increased against me. They rejoice at my troubles. Do not hide your face from Your servant: And how long will I cry out and there be no justice? When will You act in judgment against my pursuers? How many are the days of Your servant? Return Your wrath to have mercy on me. Let your kindness comfort me, please. According to Your Word to Your servant: I have recounted my ways. And from the womb, I have relied on You. Illuminate Your face upon Your servant: I am smaller than all the kindnesses. The Rock Who places the solitary in a home, which You have done with Your servant: Purify me from my sin. Do not hide Your ear to my groaning, to my cry. Please, Hashem, for I am Your servant: Show me wonders. Do not hide Your face from me. Do not turn in anger against Your servant: Turn back from Your fierce anger, and console us for the evil done to Your people.

Techinah for Thursday (Siman Shemuel):

Adonai She'eh Noded Mikino.	יְהֹוָה שְׁעֵה נוֹדֵד מִקִּנּוֹ.
Ve'orer Shenat Eino. Vayakom	וְעוֹרֵר שְׁנַת עֵינוֹ. וַיָּקָם
Bachatzi Halaylah: Mipenei	בַּחֲצִי הַלַּיְלָה: מִפְּנֵי
Boshet Ashmato. Hayetah Lo	בֹּשֶׁת אַשְׁמָתוֹ. הָיְתָה לוֹ
Dim'ato. Lechem Yomam	דִמְעָתוֹ. לֶחֶם יוֹמָם
Valaylah: Vayhi	וָלַיְלָה: וַיְהִי
Beshivyo Nehdaf. Umehar	בְּשִׁבְיוֹ נֶהְדַּף. וּמֵהַר
Legiv'ah Nirdaf. Lechorev Bayom	לְגִבְעָה נִרְדָּף. לְחֹרֶב בַּיּוֹם

Ulekerach Balaylah: Oyevim Oti	וּלְקֶרַח בַּלַּיְלָה: אוֹיְבִים אוֹתִי
Yilchatzu. Ve'alai Yitya'atzu.	יִלְחָצוּ. וְעָלַי יִתְיָעֲצוּ.
Vayitchareshu Kol	וַיִּתְחָרְשׁוּ כָּל
Halaylah: Lefaneicha Tavo	הַלַּיְלָה: לְפָנֶיךָ תָּבֹא
Tefillati. Adonai Elohei Yeshu'ati.	תְּפִלָּתִי. יְהוָה אֱלֹהֵי יְשׁוּעָתִי.
Yom Tza'akti Balaylah: Shuv	יוֹם צָעַקְתִּי בַּלַּיְלָה: שׁוּב
Mecharon Apecha, Vehinachem	מֵחֲרוֹן אַפֶּךָ. וְהִנָּחֵם
Al Hara'ah Le'ammecha:	עַל הָרָעָה לְעַמֶּךָ:

Hashem, behold the wanderer from his nest, and awaken the sleep of his eyes. And he arose in the middle of the night. Because of the shame of his guilt, his tears are his daily and nightly bread. He was scorned while captive, pursued from city to hill, by the sword during the day and the cold at night. My enemies oppress me, they conspire against me, and they were silent all night long. May my prayer come before You, Hashem, God of my salvation. I cried out day and night. Turn back from Your fierce anger, and console us for the evil done to Your people.

Techinah for Friday (Siman Avraham):

Adonai Elohim Moshiv Yechidim.	יְהוָה אֱלֹהִים מוֹשִׁיב יְחִידִים.
She'eh Le'omedim. Beveit	שְׁעֵה לְעוֹמְדִים. בְּבֵית
Adonai Balleilot: Becha Vatachti.	יְהוָה בַּלֵּילוֹת: בְּךָ בָטַחְתִּי.
Veshimcha Zacharti. Al Mishkavi	וְשִׁמְךָ זָכַרְתִּי. עַל מִשְׁכָּבִי
Balleilot: Rachem Al Holech	בַּלֵּילוֹת: רַחֵם עַל הוֹלֵךְ
Uvachoh. Ish Charbo Al Yerecho.	וּבָכֹה. אִישׁ חַרְבּוֹ עַל יְרֵכוֹ.
Mipachad Balleilot: Hini Holech	מִפַּחַד בַּלֵּילוֹת: הִנְנִי הוֹלֵךְ
Shechoach. Lo Matzati	שְׁחוֹחַ. לֹא מָצָאתִי

Manoach. Yamim Gam	מָנוֹחַ. יָמִים גַּם
Leilot: Mallet Tzo'ek Negdecha.	לֵילוֹת: מַלֵּט צוֹעֵק נֶגְדֶּךָ.
Lehagid Baboker Chasdecha.	לְהַגִּיד בַּבֹּקֶר חַסְדֶּךָ.
Ve'emunatecha Balleilot: Shuv	וֶאֱמוּנָתְךָ בַּלֵּילוֹת: שׁוּב
Mecharon Apecha, Vehinachem	מֵחֲרוֹן אַפֶּךָ. וְהִנָּחֵם
Al Hara'ah Le'ammecha:	עַל הָרָעָה לְעַמֶּךָ:

Hashem Elohim, Who settles the solitary, look upon those who stand in the house of Hashem at night. In You I trusted, and Your name I remembered upon my bed at night. Have mercy on the one who walks and weeps, a man with his sword on his thigh, from fear at night. Behold, I go bowed down, I found no rest, days and also nights. Rescue the one crying out before You, to declare Your kindness in the morning, and Your faithfulness at night. Turn back from Your fierce anger, and console us for the evil done to Your people.

Shuv Mecharon Apecha,	שׁוּב מֵחֲרוֹן אַפֶּךָ.
Vehinachem Al Hara'ah	וְהִנָּחֵם עַל הָרָעָה
Le'ammecha: Al Tiktzof Adonai	לְעַמֶּךָ: אַל תִּקְצֹף יְהֹוָה
Ad Me'od Ve'al La'ad Tizkor	עַד מְאֹד וְאַל לָעַד תִּזְכֹּר
Avon. Hen Habet Na Ammecha	עָוֹן. הֵן הַבֶּט נָא עַמְּךָ
Chullanu: Al Tin'atz Lema'an	כֻּלָּנוּ: אַל תִּנְאַץ לְמַעַן
Shemecha. Al Tenabel Kisse	שְׁמֶךָ. אַל תְּנַבֵּל כִּסֵּא
Chevodecha. Zechor Al Tafer	כְבוֹדֶךָ. זְכֹר אַל תָּפֵר
Beritcha Itanu: Im Avoneinu Anu	בְּרִיתְךָ אִתָּנוּ: אִם עֲוֹנֵינוּ עָנוּ
Banu. Adonai Aseh Lema'an	בָּנוּ. יְהֹוָה עֲשֵׂה לְמַעַן
Shemecha. Ki Rabu	שְׁמֶךָ. כִּי רַבּוּ

Meshuvoteinu Lecha Chatanu.   מְשׁוּבוֹתֵינוּ לְךָ חָטָאנוּ.

Adon Selach Lanu: אָדוֹן סְלַח לָנוּ:

Turn back from Your fierce anger, and console us for the evil done to Your people. Do not be exceedingly angry, Hashem, and do not remember our sin forever. Behold, please look upon Your people, all of us: Do not reject us for the sake of Your name. Do not discredit Your glorious throne. Remember, do not annul Your covenant with us. Even if our sins testify against us, Hashem, act for the sake of Your name. Because our backslidings are many, we have sinned against You, Lord, forgive us.

Im Ashamenu Kattola He'edim.   אִם אֲשָׁמֵנוּ כַּתּוֹלַע הָאֱדִים.

Adonai Et Hamon Rachameicha   יְהֹוָה אֶת הֲמוֹן רַחֲמֶיךָ

Takdim. Lema'an Av Mutzal   תַּקְדִּים. לְמַעַן אָב מֻצָּל

Mikasdim. Gibarto Be'emek   מִכַּשְׂדִּים. גִּבַּרְתּוֹ בְּעֵמֶק

Hasiddim. Ahavato Zechor   הַשִּׂדִּים. אַהֲבָתוֹ זְכֹר

Hayom Lanu. Ki Rabu   הַיּוֹם לָנוּ. כִּי רַבּוּ

Meshuvoteinu Lecha Chatanu.   מְשׁוּבוֹתֵינוּ לְךָ חָטָאנוּ.

Adon Selach Lanu: אָדוֹן סְלַח לָנוּ:

If our sins are red like a scarlet worm, Hashem, multiply Your mercies ahead of us. For the sake of our father (Avraham) who was saved from [Ur] Kasdim, who proved his strength in the valley of Siddim. Remember his love for us today. Because our backslidings are many, we have sinned against You, Lord, forgive us.

Im Chatanu Vehirbinu Latzon.   אִם חָטָאנוּ וְהִרְבִּינוּ לָצוֹן.

Adonai Galleh Lanu Et Ratzon.   יְהֹוָה גַּלֵּה לָנוּ עֵת רָצוֹן.

Lema'an Dagul Hane'ekad   לְמַעַן דָּגוּל הַנֶּעֱקַד

Katzon. Ve'ayil Hushat Kofro   כַּצֹּאן. וְאַיִל הוּשַׁת כָּפְרוֹ

Leratzon. Akedato Zechor   לְרָצוֹן. עֲקֵדָתוֹ זְכֹר

Hayom Lanu. Ki Rabu   הַיּוֹם לָנוּ. כִּי רַבּוּ

Meshuvoteinu Lecha Chatanu.   מְשׁוּבוֹתֵינוּ לְךָ חָטָאנוּ.

Adon Selach Lanu: אָדוֹן סְלַח לָנוּ:

If we have sinned and increasingly mocked, Hashem, reveal to us a time of favor. For the sake of the chosen one (Yitzchak) who was bound like a sheep, and the ram was offered in substitution favorably. Remember his binding today for us. Because our backslidings are many, we have sinned against You, Lord, forgive us.

Im Hirbinu Pesha Va'averah.   אִם הִרְבִּינוּ פֶּשַׁע וַעֲבֵרָה.

Adonai Hitratzeh Ba'atirah.   יְהֹוָה הִתְרַצֵּה בַּעֲתִירָה.

Lema'an Tam Chazah Sullam   לְמַעַן תָּם חָזָה סֻלָּם

Vayira. Velan Bamakom Mah   וַיִּירָא. וְלָן בַּמָּקוֹם מַה

Nora. Tumato Zechor Hayom   נּוֹרָא. תֻּמָּתוֹ זְכֹר הַיּוֹם

Lanu. Ki Rabu Meshuvoteinu   לָנוּ. כִּי רַבּוּ מְשׁוּבוֹתֵינוּ

Lecha Chatanu. Adon Selach   לְךָ חָטָאנוּ. אָדוֹן סְלַח

Lanu: לָנוּ:

If we have many transgressions and wrongdoing, Hashem, be pleased with our supplication. For the sake of the innocent one (Yaakov) who saw the ladder and was afraid, and who slept in a place so awesome. Remember his innocence today for us. Because our backslidings are many, we have sinned against You, Lord, forgive us.

Atanu Lechallot Paneicha. Ki	אָתָאנוּ לְחַלּוֹת פָּנֶיךָ. כִּי
Chesed Ve'emet Yekaddemu	חֶסֶד וֶאֱמֶת יְקַדְּמוּ
Faneicha. Na Al Tevishenu. Na	פָנֶיךָ. נָא אַל תְּבִישֵׁנוּ. נָא
Al Teshivenu Reikam	אַל תְּשִׁיבֵנוּ רֵיקָם
Millefaneicha. Selach Lanu.	מִלְּפָנֶיךָ. סְלַח לָנוּ.
Ushelach Lanu. Yeshu'ah	וּשְׁלַח לָנוּ. יְשׁוּעָה
Verachamim Mime'onecha:	וְרַחֲמִים מִמְּעוֹנֶךָ:

We have come to plead before you, for kindness and truth are
always before You. Please do not shame us; please do not turn us
back empty-handed from before You. Forgive us, and send us
salvation and mercy from Your abode.

Atanu Levakesh Mimecha	אָתָאנוּ לְבַקֵּשׁ מִמְּךָ
Kapparah. Ayom Venora. Misgav	כַּפָּרָה. אָים וְנוֹרָא. מִשְׂגָּב
Le'itot Batzarah. Techayeinu.	לְעִתּוֹת בַּצָּרָה. תְּחַיֵּינוּ.
Techonenu. Uveshimcha Nikra.	תְּחָנֵּנוּ. וּבְשִׁמְךָ נִקְרָא.
Selach Lanu. Ushelach Lanu.	סְלַח לָנוּ. וּשְׁלַח לָנוּ.
Yeshu'ah Verachamim	יְשׁוּעָה וְרַחֲמִים
Mime'onecha:	מִמְּעוֹנֶךָ:

We have come to request atonement from You. Terrifying and
Awesome One, Stronghold in times of distress, give us life and be
gracious to us and we shall call on Your name. Forgive us, and send
us salvation and mercy from Your abode.

Continue with Marina Devishmaya on the next page.

Marana Devishmaya

Marana Devishmaya. Lach	מָרָנָא דְבִשְׁמַיָּא. לָךְ
Mitchanenan Ke'avda	מִתְחַנְּנָן כְּעַבְדָּא
Demitchanen Lemareh. Hav Lan	דְּמִתְחַנֵּן לְמָארֵהּ. הַב לָן
Liba Letiyuveta. Vela Nehdar	לִבָּא לִתְיוּבְתָּא. וְלָא נֶהְדַּר
Reikam Min Kamach:	רֵיקָם מִן קַמָּךְ:

Our Master in the heavens, we supplicate to You like a slave supplicating to his master – give us the heart to repent, and do not send us away empty-handed from before You.

Marana Devishmaya. Lach	מָרָנָא דְבִשְׁמַיָּא. לָךְ
Mitchanenan Kevar Shivya	מִתְחַנְּנָן כְּבַר שִׁבְיָא
Demitchanen Lemareh. Kullehon	דְּמִתְחַנֵּן לְמָארֵהּ. כֻּלְּהוֹן
Benei Shivya Bechaspa	בְּנֵי שִׁבְיָא בְּכַסְפָּא
Mitparekin. Ve'ammach Beit	מִתְפָּרְקִין. וְעַמָּךְ בֵּית
Yisra'el Bitzlotin Uvetachanunin.	יִשְׂרָאֵל בִּצְלוֹתִין וּבְתַחֲנוּנִין.
Arem Yeminach Ve'atzmach	אָרֵם יְמִינָךְ וְאַצְמַח
Purkanach. Sivra Dechayaya	פֻּרְקָנָךְ. סִבְרָא דְחַיָּיא
Umetaya: Mitratzeh	וּמֵתַיָּא: מִתְרַצֶּה
Berachamim. Umitpayes	בְּרַחֲמִים. וּמִתְפַּיֵּס
Betachanunim. Hitratzeh	בְּתַחֲנוּנִים. הִתְרַצֵּה
Vehitpayes. Le'am Ani	וְהִתְפַּיֵּס. לְעַם עָנִי
Umeduldal. Perokana	וּמְדֻלְדָּל. פְּרוֹקָנָא
Deme'alema Meshezevana	דְּמֵעָלְמָא מְשֵׁזְבָנָא
Demillekadmin. Perok Ya'akov	דְּמִלְּקַדְמִין. פְּרֹק יַעֲקֹב
Me'ar'a Rechika. Ve'assik Zar'eh	מֵאַרְעָא רְחִיקָא. וְאַסִּיק זַרְעֵהּ
Me'ar'a Deshivya:	מֵאַרְעָא דְשִׁבְיָא:

Our Master in the heavens, we supplicate to You like a captive supplicating his master. All of the captives are redeemed with money, but Your people, the House of Yisrael, are redeemed with prayers and with supplications. Raise Your right [hand] and let Your redemption break forth. You are the Hope of the living and the dead. He Who reconciles with mercy and appeases with supplications, reconcile and appease the poor and destitute people. Redeemer from ancient times, the Refuge of olden days, redeem Yaakov from faraway lands and extract his offspring from a land of captivity.

Machei Umassei. Memit	מַחֵי וּמַסֵּי. מְמִית
Umechei. Massik Min She'ol	וּמֵחֵי. מַסִּיק מִן שְׁאוֹל
Lechayei Alema: Bera Kad	לְחַיֵּי עָלְמָא: בְּרָא כַּד
Chatei. Avuhi Lakyeh. Avuhi	חָטֵי. אֲבוּהִי לַקְיֵהּ. אֲבוּהִי
Dechayis. Assei Lecheveh: Avda	דְחַיִּיס. אַסֵּי לְכַאבֵהּ: עַבְדָּא
Demarid. Venafik Bekolar.	דְּמָרִיד. וְנָפִיק בְּקוֹלָר.
Lemareh Ta'iv. Yitbar Kolareh.	לְמָאֲרֵהּ תָּאִיב. יִתְבַּר קוֹלָרֵהּ.
Berach Buchrach Anan.	בְּרַךְ בְּכְרַךְ אֲנָן.
Vechateinan Kamach. Ha Ravya	וְחַטֵּינָן קַמָּךְ. הָא רַוְיָא
Nafshin. Begiddin Umeradin: Ha	נַפְשִׁין. בְּגִדִּין וּמְרָדִין: הָא
Avdach Anan. Umeraddenan	עַבְדָּךְ אֲנָן. וּמְרַדְּנָן
Kamach. Ha Bevizta Veshivya.	קַמָּךְ. הָא בְּבִזְתָּא וְשִׁבְיָא.
Veha Bemalkiyuta: Beva'u	וְהָא בְּמַלְקִיּוּתָא: בְּבָעוּ
Minach. Bematu Minach.	מִנָּךְ. בְּמָטוּ מִנָּךְ.
Berachamach Dinfishin. Assei	בְּרַחֲמָךְ דְּנִפְשִׁין. אַסֵּי
Lechevin. De'itekafu Alan. Ad	לְכַאבִין. דְּאִתְקַפוּ עֲלָן. עַד
Dela Nehevei. Gemira Beshivya:	דְּלָא נֶהֱוֵי. גְּמִירָא בְּשִׁבְיָא:
Machei Umassei. Memit	

Umechei. Massik Min She'ol

מַחֲי וּמַסֵּי. מֵמִית וּמְחֵי. מַסִּיק

Lechayei Alema:

מִן שְׁאוֹל לְחַיֵּי עָלְמָא:

The One Who afflicts and Who heals, the One Who takes life and revives, Who brings up from the grave to eternal life – When a son sins, his father strikes him; a father who is compassionate soothes his pain. A slave that rebels and is put in chains; when he repents to his master, he removes his chains. We are Your firstborn son, and we have sinned before You, we have been sated with harshness and bitterness. We are Your slaves, and we have rebelled before You, we are looted and captured, and lashed. We plead of You, we implore You, In Your great mercy, heal the pains that are afflicted on us before we will not survive in captivity. The One Who afflicts and Who heals, the One Who takes life and revives, Who brings up from the grave to eternal life.

Rachamim Peshutim Bikashnu

רַחֲמִים פְּשׁוּטִים בִּקַּשְׁנוּ

Mimach. Ki Rabbim Rachamim

מִמְּךָ. כִּי רַבִּים רַחֲמִים

Imach. Tzedakah Vachesed Aseh

עִמָּךָ. צְדָקָה וָחֶסֶד עֲשֵׂה

Imanu Lema'an Shemecha. Ana

עִמָּנוּ לְמַעַן שְׁמֶךָ. אָנָּא

Adonai Eloheinu Haser Mimenu

יְהֹוָה אֱלֹהֵינוּ הָסֵר מִמֶּנּוּ

Umibatteinu. Umibattei Chol

וּמִבָּתֵּינוּ. וּמִבָּתֵּי כָל

Ammecha Beit Yisra'el Bechol

עַמְּךָ בֵּית יִשְׂרָאֵל בְּכָל

Makom Shehem. Dever.

מָקוֹם שֶׁהֵם. דֶּבֶר.

Vecherev. Vera'ah. Vera'av.

וְחֶרֶב. וְרָעָה. וְרָעָב.

Ushevi. Uvizah. Umashchit.

וּשְׁבִי. וּבִזָּה. וּמַשְׁחִית.

Umaggefah. Vesatan. Veyetzer

וּמַגֵּפָה. וְשָׂטָן. וְיֵצֶר

Hara. Vechola'im Ra'im. Vetzar.

הָרַע. וְחוֹלָאִים רָעִים. וְצַר.

Me'ammacha:

מֵעַמְּךָ:

Simple mercy we have requested from You, for much mercy is with You. Perform righteousness and kindness with us for the sake of Your name. Please, Hashem our God, take away from us and from our houses and from the houses of all Your people, Yisrael, in all places where they are – pestilence, war, evil, famine, captivity, looting, destruction, plague, the adversary, the evil inclination, bad diseases and distress from Your people.

Chayim Tovim Sha'alnu	חַיִּים טוֹבִים שָׁאַלְנוּ
Mimach. Ki Mekor Chayim	מִמָּךְ. כִּי מְקוֹר חַיִּים
Imach. Tzedakah Vachesed Aseh	עִמָּךְ. צְדָקָה וָחֶסֶד עֲשֵׂה
Imanu Lema'an Shemecha. Ana	עִמָּנוּ לְמַעַן שְׁמֶךְ. אָנָּא
Adonai Eloheinu Haser Mimenu	יְהֹוָה אֱלֹהֵינוּ הָסֵר מִמֶּנּוּ
Umibatteinu. Umibattei Chol	וּמִבָּתֵּינוּ. וּמִבָּתֵּי כָל
Ammecha Beit Yisra'el Bechol	עַמְּךָ בֵּית יִשְׂרָאֵל בְּכָל
Makom Shehem. Dever.	מָקוֹם שֶׁהֵם. דֶּבֶר.
Vecherev. Vera'ah. Vera'av.	וְחֶרֶב. וְרָעָה. וְרָעָב.
Ushevi. Uvizah. Umashchit.	וּשְׁבִי. וּבִזָּה. וּמַשְׁחִית.
Umaggefah. Vesatan. Veyetzer	וּמַגֵּפָה. וְשָׂטָן. וְיֵצֶר
Hara. Vechola'im Ra'im. Vetzar.	הָרָע. וְחוֹלָאִים רָעִים. וְצַר.
Me'ammacha:	מֵעַמְּךָ:

Good life have we asked of You, for the source of life is with You. Perform righteousness and kindness with us for the sake of Your name. Please, Hashem our God, take away from us and from our houses and from the houses of all Your people, Yisrael, in all places where they are – pestilence, war, evil, famine, captivity, looting, destruction, plague, the adversary, the evil inclination, bad diseases and distress from Your people.

Eleicha Adonai

Eleicha Adonai Nasati Einai.	אֵלֶיךָ יְהוָה נָשָׂאתִי עֵינִי.
Shema Kol Tachanunai. Kegodel	שְׁמַע קוֹל תַּחֲנוּנִי. כְּגֹדֶל
Chasdecha: Beshimcha Batachti.	חַסְדֶּךָ: בְּשִׁמְךָ בָּטַחְתִּי.
Vechapai Shittachti. Devarim	וְכַפַּי שִׁטַחְתִּי. דְּבָרִים
Lakachti. Uvati Adeicha: Gaveru	לָקַחְתִּי. וּבָאתִי עָדֶיךָ: גָּבְרוּ
Yegonotai. Vayirbu Anchotai. Ki	יְגוֹנוֹתַי. וַיִּרְבּוּ אַנְחוֹתַי. כִּי
Chol Avonotai. Shattah	כָל עֲוֹנוֹתַי. שַׁתָּה
Lenegdecha: Dalefah Mitugah.	לְנֶגְדֶּךָ: דָּלְפָה מִתּוּגָה.
Nafshi Ha'anugah. Vechalletz	נַפְשִׁי הָעֲנוּגָה. וְחַלֵּץ
Mide'agah. Nefesh Avdecha:	מִדְּאָגָה. נֶפֶשׁ עַבְדֶּךָ:
Ha'aver Chatati. Elohei Yeshu'ati.	הַעֲבֵר חַטָּאתִי. אֱלֹהֵי יְשׁוּעָתִי.
Vegam Et Dim'ati. Simah	וְגַם אֶת דִּמְעָתִי. שִׂימָה
Benodecha: Uverogez Rachem.	בְּנֹאדֶךָ: וּבְרֹגֶז רַחֵם.
Zacherah Vehinachem.	זָכְרָה וְהִנָּחֵם.
Vesameach Venachem. Nefesh	וְשַׂמֵּחַ וְנַחֵם. נֶפֶשׁ
Avdecha: Zechor Aneyi	עַבְדֶּךָ: זְכֹר עָנְיִי
Umerudi. La'anah Me'odi. Ad	וּמְרוּדִי. לַעֲנָה מְעוֹדִי. עַד
Matai Lenegdi. Techadesh	מָתַי לְנֶגְדִּי. תְּחַדֵּשׁ
Edeicha: Cherefuni Tzorerai.	עֵדֶיךָ: חֵרְפוּנִי צוֹרְרָי.
Oyevai Veshorerai. Hakshev Na	אוֹיְבַי וְשׁוֹרְרָי. הַקְשֵׁב נָא
Amarai. Bevo'i Befachdecha:	אֲמָרַי. בְּבֹאִי בְּפַחְדֶּךָ:
Tamenu Li Zedim. Pachim	טָמְנוּ לִי זֵדִים. פַּחִים
Umetzudim. Uvahem Nilkadim.	וּמְצוּדִים. וּבָהֶם נִלְכָּדִים.
Pa'amei Yedideicha: Yesimun Li	פַּעֲמֵי יְדִידֶיךָ: יְשִׂימוּן לִי
Metzudim. Vesheker Bi Me'idim.	מְצוּדִים. וְשֶׁקֶר בִּי מְעִידִים.
Be'aluni Zedim. Tzur,	בְּעָלוּנִי זֵדִים. צוּר.

Bil'adeicha: Kevodecha Galleh	בִּלְעָדֶיךָ: כְּבוֹדְךָ גַּלֵּה
Tzur. Le'am Azuv Ve'atzur.	צוּר. לְעַם עָזוּב וְעָצוּר.
Vetuvecha Hanatzur. Tenah	וְטוּבְךָ הַנָּצוּר. תְּנָה
Lisrideicha: Lechutzim Berov	לִשְׂרִידֶיךָ: לְחוּצִים בְּרֹב
Dochak. Mehem Al Tirchak.	דֹּחַק. מֵהֶם אַל תִּרְחַק.
Zechor Le'avraham Leyitzchak.	זְכֹר לְאַבְרָהָם לְיִצְחָק.
Uleyisra'el Avadeicha: Marom	וּלְיִשְׂרָאֵל עֲבָדֶיךָ: מָרוֹם
Mimeromim. Rachem Al	מִמְּרוֹמִים. רַחֵם עַל
Agumim. Ve'al Zera Rechumim.	עֲגוּמִים. וְעַל זֶרַע רְחוּמִים.
Yelidei Yedideicha: No'akim	יְלִידֵי יְדִידֶיךָ: נוֹאֲקִים
Bevor Galut. Becha Samu Eyalut.	בְּבוֹר גָּלוּת. בְּךָ שָׂמוּ אֱיָלוּת.
Veharem Mishiflut. Geza	וְהָרֵם מִשִּׁפְלוּת. גֶּזַע
Chasideicha: Sovelei Ol	חֲסִידֶיךָ: סוֹבְלֵי עֹל
Tetzahel. Ve'oyeveihem Tevahel.	תְּצַהֵל. וְאוֹיְבֵיהֶם תְּבַהֵל.
Uchekedem Tenahel.	וּכְקֶדֶם תְּנַהֵל.
Syrian Congregations: Diglei Hamoneicha:	קהלות סוריות: דִּגְלֵי הֲמוֹנֶיךָ:
Other Congregations: Diglei	קהלות אחרות: דִּגְלֵי
Gedudeicha: Aneh Et Atiratam.	גְדוּדֶיךָ: עֲנֵה אֶת עֲתִירָתָם.
Semoch Et Nefilatam. Vehashev	סְמֹךְ אֶת נְפִילָתָם. וְהָשֵׁב
Et Shevutam. Me'afsei	אֶת שְׁבוּתָם. מֵאַפְסֵי
Cheldecha: Pedeh Am Lecha	חֶלְדֶּךָ: פְּדֵה עַם לְךָ
Homeh. Uche'illem Domeh.	הוֹמֶה. וּכְאִלֵּם דּוֹמֶה.
Begalut Zeh Chameh. Save'u	בְּגָלוּת זֶה כַמֶּה. שָׂבְעוּ
Nedudeicha: Tzaddik Bemif'alot.	נְדוּדֶיךָ: צַדִּיק בְּמִפְעָלוֹת.
Lecha Nitkenu Alilot. Delenu	לְךָ נִתְכְּנוּ עֲלִילוֹת. דְּלֵנוּ
Mimetzulot. Lema'an	מִמְּצוּלוֹת. לְמַעַן
Chasadeicha: Kabetz Mefuzarim.	חֲסָדֶיךָ: קַבֵּץ מְפֻזָּרִים.

Bechavlei Tzar Segurim. Bela'um	בְּכַבְלֵי צַר סְגוּרִים. בְּלָעוּם
Achzarim. Sarefu Mo'adeicha:	אַכְזָרִים. שָׂרְפוּ מוֹעֲדֶיךָ:
Rachum Heyeh Lemish'an.	רַחוּם הֱיֵה לְמִשְׁעָן.
Le'am Raveh La'an. Va'aseh Na	לְעַם רְוֵה לַעַן. וַעֲשֵׂה נָא
Lema'an. Sheloshet Avadeicha:	לְמַעַן. שְׁלֹשֶׁת עֲבָדֶיךָ:
Shaddai Nisgavta. Bechol Asher	שַׁדַּי נִשְׂגַּבְתָּ. בְּכָל אֲשֶׁר
Pa'alta. Ki Tzaddik Attah.	פָּעַלְתָּ. כִּי צַדִּיק אַתָּה.
Vetzedek Maddeicha: Techaper	וְצֶדֶק מַדֶּיךָ: תְּכַפֵּר
Avoni Ki. Sivri Becha Malki.	עֲוֹנִי כִּי. שִׂבְרִי בָךְ מַלְכִּי.
Vechonen Et Darki. Elohai	וְכוֹנֵן אֶת דַּרְכִּי. אֱלֹהַי
Le'avedecha: Tish'eh Litfillati.	לְעַבְדֶּךָ: תִּשְׁעֵה לִתְפִלָּתִי.
Ulesiach Rinati. Ki Attah Tikvati.	וּלְשִׂיחַ רִנָּתִי. כִּי אַתָּה תִקְוָתִי.
Umi Lo Ye'idecha: Eleicha	וּמִי לֹא יְעִידֶךָ: אֵלֶיךָ
Adonai Nasati Einai. Shema Kol	יְהֹוָה נָשָׂאתִי עֵינַי. שְׁמַע קוֹל
Tachanunai. Kegodel Chasdecha:	תַּחֲנוּנַי. כְּגֹדֶל חַסְדֶּךָ:

To You, Hashem, I have lifted my eyes; listen to the voice of my supplications according to Your great kindness. In Your name I have trusted, and I have spread my hands (in prayer); I have taken words and come to You. My sorrow has become overwhelming, and my sighing great, since all of my iniquities are placed in front of You. Racked with grief is my delicate soul, and rescue from worry the soul of Your servant. Take away my sin, God of my salvation; and also place my tears into Your vessel. And in anger, have mercy, remember and reconsider; and make happy and console the soul of Your servant. Recall my poverty and misery, and bitterness since I existed; How long will You renew Your witnesses against me? Cursed have I been by my attackers, my enemies and my oppressors. Listen please to my words when I come in fear. Wicked ones have hidden for me traps and snares; and captured by the feet of Your beloved. They have set traps for me, and testify falsehood against me; the arrogant would swallow me, my Rock, without You. Reveal Your glory, Rock, to a people forsaken and captive; and Your hidden goodness give to Your remnant. Those pressured by much stress, from them do not distance Yourself; remember for Avraham, Yitzchak and Yisrael, Your servants. Most High, have mercy upon the distraught and upon the seed of the ones that were granted mercy, the children of Your beloved. Groaning from the pit of exile, they have placed their acclamation with You; so bring up the seed of Your pious ones from lowliness. Make the carriers of the yoke [of exile] rejoice, and confuse their enemies; and as in the past, lead Other Congregations: the flags of Your formations. Syrian Congregations: the flags of Your multitudes. Answer their entreaties, support their fallen; and bring back their captives from the ends of Your world. Redeem the nation that yearns for You; yet like a mute in the exile, how much have Your wanderers endured. Righteous in deeds, for You measured actions; Bring us up from the depths for the sake of Your pious ones. Gather the dispersed ones, in the shackles of the foe they are enchained; cruel ones have swallowed them, they have burnt Your places of meeting. Merciful One, be a Support for the nation sated with wormwood; and do it for the sake of Your three servants. Shaddai, You are mighty in everything You have done; as You are righteous and Your garb is righteousness. Cleanse my iniquity, for my anticipation is with You, my King; and set forth my path, my God, to serve You. Accept my prayer and the speech of my hymn, as You are my hope; and who would not testify to Your Unity. To You, Hashem, I have lifted my eyes; listen to the sound of my supplications according to Your great kindness.

Continue on the next page with Avinu Av Harachaman.

אָבִינוּ אָב הָרַחֲמָן. וְהוֹשִׁיעֵנוּ לְמַעַן שְׁמֶךָ:

Avinu Av Harachaman, VeHoshi'enu Lema'an Shemecha:

Our Father, the merciful Father, save us for the sake of Your name.

אֱלֹהֵינוּ וֵאלֹהֵי אֲבוֹתֵינוּ. וְהוֹשִׁיעֵנוּ לְמַעַן שְׁמֶךָ:

Eloheinu Velohei Avoteinu, Vehoshi'enu Lema'an Shemecha:

Our God and the God of our fathers, save us for the sake of Your name.

בַּצָּר לָנוּ קְרָאנוּךָ. וְהוֹשִׁיעֵנוּ לְמַעַן שְׁמֶךָ:

Batzar Lanu Keranucha, Vehoshi'enu Lema'an Shemecha:

We have called You in our distress, save us for the sake of Your name.

גַּלְגֵּל עָלֵינוּ הֲמוֹן רַחֲמֶיךָ. וְהוֹשִׁיעֵנוּ לְמַעַן שְׁמֶךָ:

Galgel Aleinu Hamon Rachameicha, Vehoshi'enu Lema'an Shemecha:

Bring down much mercy upon us, and save us for the sake of Your name.

דְּרַשְׁנוּךָ הִמָּצֵא לָנוּ. וְהוֹשִׁיעֵנוּ לְמַעַן שְׁמֶךָ:

Derashnucha Himatze Lanu, Vehoshi'enu Lema'an Shemecha:

When we seek You, appear for us, and save us for the sake of Your name.

הֵעָתֵר לָנוּ הַיּוֹם וּבְכָל יוֹם וָיוֹם בִּתְפִלָּתֵנוּ. וְהוֹשִׁיעֵנוּ לְמַעַן שְׁמֶךָ:

He'ater Lanu Hayom Uvechol Yom Vayom Bitfillatenu, Vehoshi'enu Lema'an Shemecha:

Answer us today, and each and every day, in our prayers, and save us for the sake of Your name.

וְאַל תְּבִישֵׁנוּ מִשִּׂבְרֵנוּ. וְהוֹשִׁיעֵנוּ לְמַעַן שְׁמֶךְ:

Ve'al Tevishenu Mishioverenu, Vehoshi'enu Lema'an Shemecha:

Do not embarrass us in our hopes, and save us for the sake of Your name.

זָכְרֵנוּ בְּזִכְרוֹן טוֹב מִלְּפָנֶיךָ. וְהוֹשִׁיעֵנוּ לְמַעַן שְׁמֶךְ:

Zacherenu Bezichron Tov Millefaneicha, Vehoshi'enu Lema'an Shemecha:

Remember us for good before You, and save us for the sake of Your name.

חוּס וְרַחֵם עָלֵינוּ. וְהוֹשִׁיעֵנוּ לְמַעַן שְׁמֶךְ:

Chus Verachem Aleinu, Vehoshi'enu Lema'an Shemecha:

Pity and have mercy upon us, and save us for the sake of Your name.

טַהֲרֵנוּ מִטֻּמְאוֹת עֲוֹנֵינוּ. וְהוֹשִׁיעֵנוּ לְמַעַן שְׁמֶךְ:

Taharenu Mitum'ot Avoneinu, Vehoshi'enu Lema'an Shemecha:

Purify us from the impurities of our iniquities, and save us for the sake of Your name.

יֶהֱמוּ נָא רַחֲמֶיךָ עָלֵינוּ. וְהוֹשִׁיעֵנוּ לְמַעַן שְׁמֶךְ:

Yehemu Na Rachameicha Aleinu, Vehoshi'enu Lema'an Shemecha:

Arouse Your mercy, and save us for the sake of Your name.

חֲמֹל עַל עַמָּךְ. וְרַחֵם עַל נַחֲלָתָךְ. חוּסָה נָא כְּרֹב רַחֲמֶיךָ. חָנֵּנוּ מַלְכֵּנוּ וַעֲנֵנוּ:

Chamol Al Ammach. Verachem Al Nachalatach. Chusah Na Kerov Rachameicha. Chonenu Malkenu Va'anenu:

Have compassion on Your people and please have mercy on Your inheritance, and save us for the sake of Your name.

Some congregations say, others may skip to next:

Avinu Malkenu Avinu Attah.	אָבִינוּ מַלְכֵּנוּ אָבִינוּ אַתָּה. אָבִינוּ
Avinu Malkenu Ein Lanu Ella	מַלְכֵּנוּ אֵין לָנוּ אֶלָּא
Attah. Avinu Malkenu Rachem	אַתָּה. אָבִינוּ מַלְכֵּנוּ רַחֵם
Aleinu: Im Hetavnu Fo'al. Avinu	עָלֵינוּ: אִם הֵטַבְנוּ פֹּעַל. אָבִינוּ
Attah. Ve'im Hera'nu Ma'al. Ein	אַתָּה. וְאִם הֲרֵעְנוּ מַעַל. אֵין
Lanu Ella Attah. Avinu Malkenu	לָנוּ אֶלָּא אַתָּה. אָבִינוּ מַלְכֵּנוּ
Rachem Aleinu: Im Gavar	רַחֵם עָלֵינוּ: אִם גָּבַר
Pish'enu. Avinu Attah. Attah Tzur	פִּשְׁעֵנוּ. אָבִינוּ אַתָּה. אַתָּה צוּר
Yish'enu. Ein Lanu Ella Attah.	יִשְׁעֵנוּ. אֵין לָנוּ אֶלָּא אַתָּה.
Avinu Malkenu Rachem Aleinu:	אָבִינוּ מַלְכֵּנוּ רַחֵם עָלֵינוּ:
Im Hirbinu Omer. Avinu Attah.	אִם הִרְבִּינוּ אֹמֶר. אָבִינוּ אַתָּה.
Zechor Ki Anachnu Chomer. Ein	זְכֹר כִּי אֲנַחְנוּ חֹמֶר. אֵין
Lanu Ella Attah. Avinu Malkenu	לָנוּ אֶלָּא אַתָּה. אָבִינוּ מַלְכֵּנוּ
Rachem Aleinu: Im Lecha	רַחֵם עָלֵינוּ: אִם לָךְ
Chatanu. Avinu Attah. Adon	חָטָאנוּ. אָבִינוּ אַתָּה. אָדוֹן
Selach Lanu. Ein Lanu Ella Attah.	סְלַח לָנוּ. אֵין לָנוּ אֶלָּא אַתָּה.
Avinu Malkenu Rachem Aleinu:	אָבִינוּ מַלְכֵּנוּ רַחֵם עָלֵינוּ:
Lecha Adonai Kivinu. Avinu	לְךָ יְהֹוָה קִוִּינוּ. אָבִינוּ
Attah. Ki Attah Avinu.	אַתָּה. כִּי אַתָּה אָבִינוּ.
Ein Lanu Ella Attah. Avinu	אֵין לָנוּ אֶלָּא אַתָּה. אָבִינוּ
Malkenu Rachem Aleinu: Lecha	מַלְכֵּנוּ רַחֵם עָלֵינוּ: לְךָ
Perasnu Sha'al. Avinu Attah.	פְּרַשְׂנוּ שַׁעַל. אָבִינוּ אַתָּה.
Hamtzi Lanu Ta'al. Ein Lanu Ella	הַמְצִיא לָנוּ תַּעַל. אֵין לָנוּ אֶלָּא
Attah. Avinu Malkenu Rachem	אַתָּה. אָבִינוּ מַלְכֵּנוּ רַחֵם
Aleinu: Chushah Shelach	עָלֵינוּ: חוּשָׁה שְׁלַח
Mashiach. Avinu Attah. Vetzitz	מָשִׁיחַ. אָבִינוּ אַתָּה. וְצִיץ

Yesha Tafriach. Ein Lanu Ella	יֶשַׁע תַּפְרִיחַ. אֵין לָנוּ אֶלָּא
Attah. Avinu Malkenu Rachem	אַתָּה. אָבִינוּ מַלְכֵּנוּ רַחֵם
Aleinu: Avinu Malkenu Avinu	עָלֵינוּ: אָבִינוּ מַלְכֵּנוּ אָבִינוּ
Attah. Avinu Malkenu Ein Lanu	אַתָּה. אָבִינוּ מַלְכֵּנוּ אֵין לָנוּ
Melech Ella Attah. Avinu	מֶלֶךְ אֶלָּא אַתָּה. אָבִינוּ
Malkenu Rachem Aleinu:	מַלְכֵּנוּ רַחֵם עָלֵינוּ:

Our Father, our King, You are our Father. Our Father, our King, we have no King besides You. Our Father, our King, have mercy upon us. If we have acted well, You are our Father. And if we have done evil treachery, we have no King besides You. Our Father, our King, have mercy upon us. If our rebellion has grown, You are our Father. You are the Rock of our salvation, we have no King besides You. Our Father, our King, have mercy upon us. If we have spoken much, You are our Father. Remember that we are clay, we have no King besides You. Our Father, our King, have mercy upon us. If we have sinned to You, You are our Father. Master, forgive us, we have no King besides You. Our Father, our King, have mercy upon us. We have hoped to You, You are our Father. For You are our Father, we have no King besides You. Our Father, our King, have mercy upon us. We have spread our supplication to You, You are our Father. Who brings forth dew to us, we have no King besides You. Our Father, our King, have mercy upon us. Quickly send the Messiah, You are our Father. And may the flower of our salvation bloom, we have no King besides You. Our Father, our King, have mercy upon us. Our Father, our King, You are our Father. Our Father, our King, we have no King besides You. Our Father, our King, have mercy upon us.

Avinu Malkenu Avinu Attah.	אָבִינוּ מַלְכֵּנוּ אָבִינוּ אַתָּה.
Avinu Malkenu Ein Lanu Melech	אָבִינוּ מַלְכֵּנוּ אֵין לָנוּ מֶלֶךְ
Ella Attah. Avinu Malkenu	אֶלָּא אַתָּה. אָבִינוּ מַלְכֵּנוּ

Rachem Aleinu: Avinu Malkenu	רַחֵם עָלֵינוּ: אָבִינוּ מַלְכֵּנוּ
Chonenu Va'anenu Ki Ein Banu	חָנֵּנוּ וַעֲנֵנוּ כִּי אֵין בָּנוּ
Ma'asim. Aseh Imanu Tzedakah	מַעֲשִׂים. עֲשֵׂה עִמָּנוּ צְדָקָה
Vachesed Lema'an Shimcha	וָחֶסֶד לְמַעַן שְׁמֶךָ
Hagadol Vehoshi'enu:	הַגָּדוֹל וְהוֹשִׁיעֵנוּ:
Va'anachnu Lo Neda Mah	וַאֲנַחְנוּ לֹא נֵדַע מַה
Na'aseh Ki Aleicha Eineinu:	נַעֲשֶׂה כִּי עָלֶיךָ עֵינֵינוּ:
Zechor Rachameicha Adonai	זְכֹר רַחֲמֶיךָ יְהֹוָה
Vachasadeicha. Ki Me'olam	וַחֲסָדֶיךָ. כִּי מֵעוֹלָם
Hemah: Yehi Chasdecha Adonai	הֵמָּה: יְהִי חַסְדְּךָ יְהֹוָה
Aleinu. Ka'asher Yichalnu Lach:	עָלֵינוּ. כַּאֲשֶׁר יִחַלְנוּ לָךְ:
Al Tizkar Lanu Avonot Rishonim.	אַל תִּזְכָּר לָנוּ עֲוֹנֹת רִאשֹׁנִים.
Maher Yekaddemunu	מַהֵר יְקַדְּמוּנוּ
Rachameicha. Ki Dallonu	רַחֲמֶיךָ. כִּי דַלּוֹנוּ
Me'od: Ezrenu Beshem Adonai.	מְאֹד: עָזְרֵנוּ בְּשֵׁם יְהֹוָה.
Oseh Shamayim Va'aretz:	עוֹשֵׂה שָׁמַיִם וָאָרֶץ:
Chonenu Adonai Chonenu. Ki	חָנֵּנוּ יְהֹוָה חָנֵּנוּ. כִּי
Rav Sava'nu Vuz: Berogez	רַב שָׂבַעְנוּ בוּז: בְּרֹגֶז
Rachem Tizkor. Berogez Ahavah	רַחֵם תִּזְכֹּר. בְּרֹגֶז אַהֲבָה
Tizkor: Berogez Akedah Tizkor.	תִּזְכֹּר: בְּרֹגֶז עֲקֵדָה תִּזְכֹּר.
Berogez Temimut Tizkor. Adonai	בְּרֹגֶז תְּמִימוּת תִּזְכֹּר. יְהֹוָה
Hoshi'ah. Hamelech Ya'anenu	הוֹשִׁיעָה. הַמֶּלֶךְ יַעֲנֵנוּ
Beyom Kare'enu: Ki Hu Yada	בְּיוֹם קָרְאֵנוּ: כִּי הוּא יָדַע
Yitzrenu. Zachur Ki Afar	יִצְרֵנוּ. זָכוּר כִּי עָפָר
Anachenu: Azerenu Elohei	אֲנָחְנוּ: עָזְרֵנוּ אֱלֹהֵי
Yish'enu Al Devar Kevod	יִשְׁעֵנוּ עַל דְּבַר כְּבוֹד
Shemecha. Vehatzilenu Vechaper	שְׁמֶךָ. וְהַצִּילֵנוּ וְכַפֵּר

Al Chatoteinu Lema'an
Shemecha:

עַל חַטֹאתֵינוּ לְמַעַן
שְׁמֶךְ:

Our Father, our King, you are our Father. Our Father, our King, we have no King besides You. Our Father, our King, be gracious to us and answer us, for we have no [good] deeds. Perform righteousness and kindness with us for the sake of Your great name, and save us. And we do not know what to do, but our eyes are upon You. Remember Hashem, Your mercies, for they are eternal. Let Your kindness, Hashem, be upon us, as we have supplicated from You. Do not remember the former iniquities against us – quickly let Your mercy precede us, for we are greatly impoverished. Help us in the name of Hashem, the Creator of the heavens and the earth. Be gracious to us, Hashem, be gracious to us, for we have been sated with much disgrace. In wrath, recall mercy. In wrath, recall love. In wrath, recall the binding [of Yitzchak]. In wrath, recall innocence. Hashem, save – May the King answer on the day we call. For He knows our inclinations – remember that we are dust. Help us – God of our salvation – for the sake of Your Name's honor. And save us and atone for our sins for the sake of Your Name.

Shomer Yisra'el. Shemor She'erit
Yisra'el. Ve'al Yovad Yisra'el.
Ha'omerim Bechol Yom. Shema
Yisra'el:

שׁוֹמֵר יִשְׂרָאֵל. שְׁמֹר שְׁאֵרִית
יִשְׂרָאֵל. וְאַל יֹאבַד יִשְׂרָאֵל.
הָאוֹמְרִים בְּכָל יוֹם. שְׁמַע
יִשְׂרָאֵל:

Guardian of Yisrael, protect the remnant of Yisrael, and do not destroy Yisrael who say every day, "Shema Yisrael."

Shomer Goy Echad. Shemor שׁוֹמֵר גּוֹי אֶחָד. שְׁמֹר

She'erit Goy Echad. Ve'al Yovad שְׁאֵרִית גּוֹי אֶחָד. וְאַל יֹאבַד

Goy Echad. Ha'omerim Bechol גּוֹי אֶחָד. הָאוֹמְרִים בְּכָל

Yom. Shema Yisra'el. Adonai יוֹם. שְׁמַע יִשְׂרָאֵל. יְהֹוָה

Eloheinu. Adonai Echad: אֱלֹהֵינוּ. יְהֹוָה אֶחָד:

Guardian of the unique nation, protect the remnant of the unique nation, and do not destroy the unique nation who say every day, "Hear Oh Yisrael, Hashem is our God, Hashem is One."

Shomer Goy Kadosh. Shemor שׁוֹמֵר גּוֹי קָדוֹשׁ. שְׁמֹר

She'erit Goy Kadosh. Ve'al שְׁאֵרִית גּוֹי קָדוֹשׁ. וְאַל

Yovad Goy Kadosh. Ha'omerim יֹאבַד גּוֹי קָדוֹשׁ. הָאוֹמְרִים

Bechol Yom. Kadosh. Kadosh. בְּכָל יוֹם. קָדוֹשׁ. קָדוֹשׁ.

Kadosh: קָדוֹשׁ:

Guardian of the holy nation, protect the holy nation, and do not destroy the holy nation who say every day, "Holy, holy, holy."

Shomer Goy Rabba. Shemor שׁוֹמֵר גּוֹי רַבָּא. שְׁמֹר

She'erit Goy Rabba. Ve'al Yovad שְׁאֵרִית גּוֹי רַבָּא. וְאַל יֹאבַד

Goy Rabba. Ha'omerim Bechol גּוֹי רַבָּא. הָאוֹמְרִים בְּכָל

Yom. Amen Yehe Shemeih יוֹם. אָמֵן יְהֵא שְׁמֵיהּ

Rabba: רַבָּא:

Guardian of the great nation, protect the remnant of the great nation, and do not destroy the great nation who say every day, "Amen, May His name be great."

And the prayer leader says Kaddish Titkabbal:

Kaddish Titkabbal

Kaddish is only recited in a minyan (ten men). ᵃᵐᵉⁿ denotes when the congregation responds "Amen" together out loud. According to the Shulchan Arukh, the congregation says "Yehei Shemeh Rabba" to "Yitbarach" out loud together without interruption, and also that one should respond "Amen" after "Yitbarach." (SA, OC 55,56) This is not the common custom today. Though many are accustomed to answering according to their own custom, it is advised to respond in the custom of the one reciting to avoid not fragmenting into smaller groups. ("Lo Titgodedu" - BT, Yevamot 13b / SA, OC 493, Rema / MT, Avodah Zara 12:15)

יִתְגַּדַּל וְיִתְקַדַּשׁ שְׁמֵהּ רַבָּא. אמּן בְּעָלְמָא דִּי בְרָא. כִּרְעוּתֵהּ. וְיַמְלִיךְ מַלְכוּתֵהּ. וְיַצְמַח פֻּרְקָנֵהּ. וִיקָרֵב מְשִׁיחֵהּ. אמּן בְּחַיֵּיכוֹן וּבְיוֹמֵיכוֹן וּבְחַיֵּי דְכָל בֵּית יִשְׂרָאֵל. בַּעֲגָלָא וּבִזְמַן קָרִיב. וְאִמְרוּ אָמֵן. אמּן יְהֵא שְׁמֵהּ רַבָּא מְבָרַךְ לְעָלַם וּלְעָלְמֵי עָלְמַיָּא יִתְבָּרַךְ. וְיִשְׁתַּבַּח. וְיִתְפָּאַר. וְיִתְרוֹמַם. וְיִתְנַשֵּׂא. וְיִתְהַדָּר. וְיִתְעַלֶּה. וְיִתְהַלָּל שְׁמֵהּ דְּקֻדְשָׁא. בְּרִיךְ הוּא. אמּן לְעֵלָּא מִן כָּל בִּרְכָתָא שִׁירָתָא. תֻּשְׁבְּחָתָא וְנֶחֱמָתָא. דַּאֲמִירָן בְּעָלְמָא. וְאִמְרוּ אָמֵן. אמּן

Yitgadal Veyitkadash Shemeh Rabba. ᴬᵐᵉⁿ Be'alema Di Vera.
Kir'uteh. Veyamlich Malchuteh. Veyatzmach Purkaneh. Vikarev
Meshicheh. ᴬᵐᵉⁿ Bechayeichon Uveyomeichon Uvechayei Dechal-
Beit Yisra'el. Ba'agala Uvizman Kariv. Ve'imru Amen. ᴬᵐᵉⁿ Yehei
Shemeh Rabba Mevarach Le'alam Ule'alemei Alemaya Yitbarach.
Veyishtabach. Veyitpa'ar. Veyitromam. Veyitnasse. Veyit'hadar.
Veyit'aleh. Veyit'hallal Shemeh Dekudsha. Berich Hu. ᴬᵐᵉⁿ Le'ella
Min Kol Birchata Shirata. Tushbechata Venechemata. Da'amiran
Be'alema. Ve'imru Amen. ᴬᵐᵉⁿ

Glorified and sanctified be God's great name ᴬᵐᵉⁿ throughout the world which He has created according to His will. May He establish His kingdom, hastening His salvation and the coming of His Messiah, ᴬᵐᵉⁿ, in your lifetime and during your days, and within the life of the entire House of Yisrael, speedily and soon; and say, Amen. ᴬᵐᵉⁿ May His great name be blessed forever and to all eternity. Blessed and praised, glorified and exalted, extolled and honored, adored and lauded is the name of the Holy One, blessed is He, ᴬᵐᵉⁿ Beyond all the blessings and hymns, praises and consolations that are ever spoken in the world; and say, Amen. ᴬᵐᵉⁿ

תִּתְקַבַּל צְלוֹתָנָא וּבָעוּתָנָא. עִם צְלוֹתְהוֹן וּבָעוּתְהוֹן דְּכָל בֵּית
יִשְׂרָאֵל. קֳדָם אֲבוּנָא דְּבִשְׁמַיָּא וְאַרְעָא. וְאִמְרוּ אָמֵן. אָמֵן

Titkabbal Tzelotana Uva'utana. Im Tzelotehon Uva'utehon Dechol
Beit Yisra'el. Kodam Avuna Devishmaya Ve'ar'a. Ve'imru Amen. **Amen**

May the prayer and supplication of the whole House of Yisrael be
accepted before their Father in heaven, and say, Amen. **Amen**

יְהֵא שְׁלָמָא רַבָּא מִן שְׁמַיָּא. חַיִּים וְשָׂבָע וִישׁוּעָה וְנֶחָמָה. וְשֵׁיזָבָא
וּרְפוּאָה וּגְאוּלָה וּסְלִיחָה וְכַפָּרָה וְרֶוַח וְהַצָּלָה לָנוּ וּלְכָל עַמּוֹ
יִשְׂרָאֵל. וְאִמְרוּ אָמֵן. אָמֵן

Yehei Shelama Rabba Min Shemaya. Chayim Vesava Vishu'ah
Venechamah. Vesheizava Urefu'ah Uge'ulah Uselichah Vechaparah
Verevach Vehatzalah Lanu Ulechol Ammo Yisra'el. Ve'imru Amen.

Amen

May abundant peace descend from heaven, with life and plenty,
salvation, solace, liberation, healing and redemption, and
forgiveness and atonement, enlargement and freedom, for us and
all of God's people Yisrael; and say, Amen. **Amen**

One bows and takes three steps backwards, while still bowing. After three steps, while still bowing
and before erecting, while saying, "Oseh Shalom Bimromav", turn one's face to the left, "Hu
[Berachamav] Ya'aseh Shalom Aleinu", turn one's face to the right; then bow forward like a servant
leaving his master. (SA, OC 123:1)

עוֹשֶׂה שָׁלוֹם בִּמְרוֹמָיו. הוּא בְּרַחֲמָיו יַעֲשֶׂה שָׁלוֹם עָלֵינוּ. וְעַל
כָּל־עַמּוֹ יִשְׂרָאֵל. וְאִמְרוּ אָמֵן:

Oseh Shalom Bimromav. Hu Berachamav Ya'aseh Shalom Aleinu.
Ve'al Kol-'Ammo Yisra'el. Ve'imru Amen.

Creator of peace in His high places, may He in His mercy create
peace for us and for all Yisrael, and say Amen.

Continue with Psalms 130 on the next page.

Psalms 130

שִׁיר הַמַּעֲלוֹת. מִמַּעֲמַקִּים קְרָאתִיךָ יְהֹוָה: אֲדֹנָי שִׁמְעָה בְקוֹלִי.

תִּהְיֶינָה אָזְנֶיךָ קַשֻּׁבוֹת. לְקוֹל תַּחֲנוּנָי: אִם עֲוֹנוֹת תִּשְׁמָר יָהּ. אֲדֹנָי

מִי יַעֲמֹד: כִּי עִמְּךָ הַסְּלִיחָה. לְמַעַן תִּוָּרֵא: קִוִּיתִי יְהֹוָה קִוְּתָה נַפְשִׁי.

וְלִדְבָרוֹ הוֹחָלְתִּי: נַפְשִׁי לַאדֹנָי. מִשֹּׁמְרִים לַבֹּקֶר שֹׁמְרִים לַבֹּקֶר: יַחֵל

יִשְׂרָאֵל אֶל יְהֹוָה. כִּי עִם יְהֹוָה הַחֶסֶד. וְהַרְבֵּה עִמּוֹ פְדוּת: וְהוּא

יִפְדֶּה אֶת יִשְׂרָאֵל מִכֹּל עֲוֹנוֹתָיו:

Shir Hama'alot. Mima'amakim Keraticha Adonai: Adonai Shim'ah
Vekoli. Tihyeinah Azeneicha Kashuvot. Lekol Tachanunai: Im Avonot
Tishmar Yah. Adonai Mi Ya'amod: Ki Imecha Hasselichah. Lema'an
Tivare: Kiviti Adonai Kivetah Nafshi. Velidvaro Hochaleti: Nafshi
l'Adonai. Mishomerim Laboker Shomerim Laboker: Yachel Yisra'el El
Adonai. Ki Im Adonai Hachesed. Veharbeh Imo Fedut: Vehu Yifdeh
Et Yisra'el Mikol Avonotav:

A Song of Ascents. Out of the depths have I called You, Hashem.
Hashem, listen to my voice; let Your ears be attentive to the voice of
my supplications. If You, Hashem, should mark iniquities, Hashem,
who could stand? For with You there is forgiveness, that You may be
feared. I wait for Hashem, my soul waits, and in His word do I hope.
My soul waits for Hashem, more than watchmen for the morning,
more than watchmen for the morning. Yisrael, hope in Hashem; for
with Hashem there is mercy, and with Him is abundant redemption.
And He will redeem Yisrael from all his iniquities.

And mourners say the mourner's Kaddish (Kaddish Yehei-Shelama):

Kaddish Yehei-Shelama

Kaddish is only recited in a minyan (ten men). אמן denotes when the congregation responds "Amen" together out loud. According to the Shulchan Arukh, the congregation says "Yehei Shemeh Rabba" to "Yitbarach" out loud together without interruption, and also that one should respond "Amen" after "Yitbarach." (SA, OC 55,56) This is not the common custom today. Though many are accustomed to answering according to their own custom, it is advised to respond in the custom of the one reciting to avoid not fragmenting into smaller groups. ("Lo Titgodedu" - BT, Yevamot 13b / SA, OC 493, Rema / MT, Avodah Zara 12:15)

יִתְגַּדַּל וְיִתְקַדַּשׁ שְׁמֵהּ רַבָּא. אמן בְּעָלְמָא דִּי בְרָא. כִּרְעוּתֵהּ. וְיַמְלִיךְ
מַלְכוּתֵהּ. וְיַצְמַח פֻּרְקָנֵהּ. וִיקָרֵב מְשִׁיחֵהּ. אמן בְּחַיֵּיכוֹן וּבְיוֹמֵיכוֹן
וּבְחַיֵּי דְכָל בֵּית יִשְׂרָאֵל. בַּעֲגָלָא וּבִזְמַן קָרִיב. וְאִמְרוּ אָמֵן. אמן יְהֵא
שְׁמֵיהּ רַבָּא מְבָרַךְ לְעָלַם וּלְעָלְמֵי עָלְמַיָּא יִתְבָּרַךְ. וְיִשְׁתַּבַּח.
וְיִתְפָּאַר. וְיִתְרוֹמַם. וְיִתְנַשֵּׂא. וְיִתְהַדָּר. וְיִתְעַלֶּה. וְיִתְהַלָּל שְׁמֵהּ
דְּקֻדְשָׁא. בְּרִיךְ הוּא. אמן לְעֵלָּא מִן כָּל בִּרְכָתָא שִׁירָתָא. תֻּשְׁבְּחָתָא
וְנֶחֱמָתָא. דַּאֲמִירָן בְּעָלְמָא. וְאִמְרוּ אָמֵן. אמן

Yitgadal Veyitkadash Shemeh Rabba. ᴬᵐᵉⁿ Be'alema Di Vera.
Kir'uteh. Veyamlich Malchuteh. Veyatzmach Purkaneh. Vikarev
Meshicheh. ᴬᵐᵉⁿ Bechayeichon Uveyomeichon Uvechayei Dechal-
Beit Yisra'el. Ba'agala Uvizman Kariv. Ve'imru Amen. ᴬᵐᵉⁿ Yehei
Shemeh Rabba Mevarach Le'alam Ule'alemei Alemaya Yitbarach.
Veyishtabach. Veyitpa'ar. Veyitromam. Veyitnasse. Veyit'hadar.
Veyit'aleh. Veyit'hallal Shemeh Dekudsha. Berich Hu. ᴬᵐᵉⁿ Le'ella
Min Kol Birchata Shirata. Tushbechata Venechemata. Da'amiran
Be'alema. Ve'imru Amen. ᴬᵐᵉⁿ

Glorified and sanctified be God's great name ᴬᵐᵉⁿ throughout the
world which He has created according to His will. May He establish
His kingdom, hastening His salvation and the coming of His
Messiah, ᴬᵐᵉⁿ, in your lifetime and during your days, and within the
life of the entire House of Yisrael, speedily and soon; and say, Amen.
ᴬᵐᵉⁿ May His great name be blessed forever and to all eternity.
Blessed and praised, glorified and exalted, extolled and honored,
adored and lauded is the name of the Holy One, blessed is He, ᴬᵐᵉⁿ
Beyond all the blessings and hymns, praises and consolations that
are ever spoken in the world; and say, Amen. ᴬᵐᵉⁿ

יְהֵא שְׁלָמָא רַבָּא מִן שְׁמַיָּא. חַיִּים וְשָׂבָע וִישׁוּעָה וְנֶחָמָה. וְשֵׁיזָבָא
וּרְפוּאָה וּגְאוּלָה וּסְלִיחָה וְכַפָּרָה וְרֶוַח וְהַצָּלָה לָנוּ וּלְכָל עַמּוֹ
יִשְׂרָאֵל. וְאִמְרוּ אָמֵן. אמן

Yehei Shelama Rabba Min Shemaya. Chayim Vesava Vishu'ah
Venechamah. Vesheizava Urefu'ah Uge'ulah Uselichah
Vechapparah Verevach Vehatzalah Lanu Ulechol Ammo Yisra'el.
Ve'imru Amen. Amen

May abundant peace descend from heaven, with life and plenty,
salvation, solace, liberation, healing and redemption, and
forgiveness and atonement, enlargement and freedom, for us and
all of God's people Yisrael; and say, Amen. Amen

> One bows and takes three steps backwards, while still bowing. After three steps, while still bowing
> and before erecting, while saying, "Oseh Shalom Bimromav", turn one's face to the left, "Hu
> [Berachamav] Ya'aseh Shalom Aleinu", turn one's face to the right; then bow forward like a servant
> leaving his master. (SA, OC 123:1)

עוֹשֶׂה שָׁלוֹם בִּמְרוֹמָיו. הוּא בְּרַחֲמָיו יַעֲשֶׂה שָׁלוֹם עָלֵינוּ. וְעַל
כָּל־עַמּוֹ יִשְׂרָאֵל. וְאִמְרוּ אָמֵן:

Oseh Shalom Bimromav. Hu Berachamav Ya'aseh Shalom Aleinu.
Ve'al Kol-'Ammo Yisra'el. Ve'imru Amen.

Creator of peace in His heights, may He in His mercy create peace
for us and for all Yisrael, and say Amen.

41432427R00067

Made in the USA
Columbia, SC
02 September 2024